A TREATISE CONCERNING POLITICAL ENQUIRY AND THE LIBERTY OF THE PRESS

A Da Capo Press Reprint Series

CIVIL LIBERTIES IN AMERICAN HISTORY

GENERAL EDITOR: LEONARD W. LEVY

Claremont Graduate School

A TREATISE CONCERNING POLITICAL ENQUIRY AND THE LIBERTY OF THE PRESS

BY TUNIS WORTMAN

DA CAPO PRESS • NEW YORK • 1970

A Da Capo Press Reprint Edition

This Da Capo Press edition of *A Treatise Concerning Political
Enquiry and the Liberty of the Press* is an unabridged republica-
tion of the first edition published in New York in 1800.
It is reprinted from an original edition
owned by the Harvard Law School Library.

Library of Congress Catalog Card Number 78-122162

SBN 306-71967-3

Published by Da Capo Press
A Division of Plenum Publishing Corporation
227 West 17th Street, New York, N.Y. 10011

Manufactured in the United States of America

A

TREATISE,

CONCERNING

POLITICAL ENQUIRY,

AND THE

LIBERTY OF THE PRESS.

By TUNIS WORTMAN,

COUNSELLOR AT LAW.

———

——— POPULUMQUE FALSIS DEDOCET UTI

VOCIBUS ———   HORACE.

NEW-YORK:

PRINTED BY GEORGE FORMAN, NO. 64, WATER-STREET,

FOR THE AUTHOR.

=

1 8 0 0.

Contents.

CHAPTER I.

INTRODUCTION.

A<small>LL</small> *science originates in principles—
Genuine sphere of government—Source of moral
and social obligation—Of morality and politics—
Whether politics is a proper subject of general enquiry ?—Improvement of other sciences—Led to
the improvement of politics—Subject proposed.*

CHAP. II.

On the general right to investigate Politi-
cal Topics.

*Reciprocity of human duties—Theory of civil
society—Nature of government—Principle of responsibleness—Fallibility of government.*

CHAP. III.

The subject continued.

*Theory of mind—Philosophy of human con-
duct—Of the passions—Knowledge their only
corrective—Society the parent of the sciences.*

CHAP. IV.

On the competency of society to investigate Political Topics.

The question proposed—Similarity of human talents—Philosopher and peasant contrasted—Theories respecting the diversity of talents—Attempted to be reconciled—Philosopher and peasant compared—Of the moral sense—Government no monopolist of wisdom—Human faculties improvable—General capacity of distinguishing between virtue and vice.

CHAP. V.

The subject continued.

Enquiry respecting government—Government founded in morals—An objection—Answered—Judgment a common attribute—Distinct from genius—Nature of political subjects—Private and public morality—Identical—Application.

CHAP. VI.

The subject continued.

Ordinary detail of government—I. Internal regulation—Nature of legislative authority—Of human action—Genuine province of the legislator—An example—Duty of the legislator—II. External transactions—War—Aggression—Defence—Negotiation—Treaties—Of peace—Of alliance—Defensive—Offensive—Of commerce—Law of

CHAP. VII.

The subject continued.

CHAP. VIII.

On the perfect right of Individuals to com-municate their sentiments upon Political Topics.

CHAP. IX.

The same subject considered from the re-visionary powers of society.

CHAP. XIII.

The freedom of investigation considered as a preventative of revolution.

Horrors of revolution—Lead to a prejudicial conclusion—Progress of reason the most effectual preventative—-Vindication of the advocate of liberty.

CHAP. XIV.

The preceding subjects considered with relation to representative governments.

Theory of representation—Limitation of the elective privilege—Vindicated—Opposed—Question undecided—Of property—Investigation essential—As it respects the candidate—As it respects the elector—Restriction unsalutary and repugnant.

CHAP. XV.

The same subjects considered with relation to the Constitution of the United States.

Historical outlines of the confederation—Summary of the legislative powers of Congress—Reasoning from such premises—Summary of judicial powers—Reasoning therefrom.

CHAP. XVI.

Upon the Press, considered as a vehicle of communication.

Its importance—Its peculiar advantages in the discussion of subjects—Its influence upon government, manners, and morals—Subject to be influenced by government—Danger arising from criminal coercion—Doctrine respecting libels—Its injustice—Public and private prosecutions for libels—The latter sufficient to answer every salutary purpose—Remarks of Lord Lyttleton—On licensing the press—Additional remarks of Lord Lyttleton.

CHAP. XVII.

CONCLUSION.

On the means of Improvement.

The interference of government inadmissible—Literary associations—Intercourse of sentiment—Vehicles of communication—Education—Office of the preceptor—Conclusion.

A TREATISE, &c.

CHAPTER I.

𝔍ntroduction.

*All science originates in principles—Genuine
sphere of government—Source of moral and
social obligation—Of morality and politics—
Whether politics is a proper subject of general
enquiry ?—Improvement of other sciences—
Led to the improvement of politics—Subject
proposed.*

CHAP. I.

Eᴠᴇʀʏ science is founded in
certain primary and established principiæ ; upon
the truth and solidity of which it's existence depends.   To those governing principles, it is always necessary to resort whenever any question
arises, with respect to subjects, in which such
science is conversant, because they form the original elements of which the science is composed, and constitute the foundation upon which
the superstructure is erected.   Without an accurate and comprehensive conception of its ele-

Science
originates
in princi-
ples.

mentary principles, we can never become the masters of any branch of knowledge : the few ideas we may happen to possess, will be loose, evanescent, and unconnected. We will neither be able to reflect with accuracy, nor to reason with perspicuity or energy.

Like every other science, that of government is also founded upon peculiar and appropriate principles. Perhaps there are few subjects with respect to which we can reason with more correctness and certitude, than those which are comprehended within the general denomination of morals. Considered as a part of the extensive science of ethics, the theory of society, and the philosophy of political institution, are entitled to particular attention. There is no topic of investigation in which the happiness of mankind is more immediately concerned, than in the doctrines which relate to civil government : there is none in which the exercise of talents can be rendered more extensively beneficial.

Genuine sphere of government.
The genuine operation of government is to promote and perpetuate the happiness of a people. Political institution should emphatically be considered as that science which proposes for its object the promotion of general felicity. As government is a subject of universal concern, it should likewise become the subject of universal contemplation.

Considered as the constant objects of moral
and social obligation, we should carefully endeavour to investigate the principles and explore
the sources from which that obligation originates. The duties of a percipient being appear
to arise from the various relations in which he is
placed with regard to others. Our natural duties emanate from our natural relations—our social duties commence in our social connections.

The field of moral obligation is unlimited in
its extent—it embraces not only the universal
brotherhood of man, but comprehends within
its boundless sphere, every being that is capable of pleasure and enjoyment ; or that is susceptible of misery and pain.

The theatre of social obligation, though more
limited and circumscribed, is equally important and interesting. It exhibits *man* as modified by the habits of civil life—ameliorated by
the influence of civilization and the sciences—
regulated by the various gradations of political
subordination, and governed by the laws and
institutions of society. That science which pro-
fesses to treat of our universal obligations, is
known by the general appellation of *ethics,* or
morality : the science which investigates and
enforces our social duties, is distinguished by
the more circumscribed denomination, *politics.*

CHAP. I.
It has been made a question. of the most extensive importance to the happiness of the human race, Whether politics is a subject that may
safely be submited to the eye of popular enquiry and inspection ? And whether the mysterious arcana of State affairs should not be assiduously confined within the impenetrable recesses of the castle ? It has been practically maintained by the advocates of mystery, that a people can only be governed by stratagem and imposture ; that they will cease to retain a proper
reverence for their public institutions, the moment the hand which conducts the machine is
rendered visible. The valuable fabric of society (it has been contended) can be maintained no longer, than while the plans of the artist
and the orders of its architecture, are covered
and protected by the gloomy clouds of obscurity ; while it is the eternal destiny of the human
species to be governed by the delusion of their
senses, and not by the conviction of their understanding. Such has been the language which
has hitherto perpetuated the existence of despotism, and such the sentiments that have imped-
ed the progressive improvement of society.

Labouring under such a load of infatuation
and prejudice, it cannot excite our surprise that
the study of politics is yet in a state of infancy.
In proportion as the temple of enquiry has been
opened to mankind, their faculties have been

Whether
politics is
a proper
subject of
general
enquiry?

multiplied, and their knowledge has increased.
If other sciences, more abstract and more difficult than government, have advanced towards
an earlier state of maturity and perfection, it
is because their relation to the mysteries of State,
being indirect and undiscovered, they did not
arouse the jealousy and awaken the apprehensions of the conductors of the cabinet. Happi-
ly it was not perceived to be the prerogative of
knowledge, to extend her empire, and to dart
her inquisitive glance into every region of contemplation. It was yet unknown to Princes,
that all the sciences * are united by the closest
ties of consanguinity, and that the perfection of
one inevitably points to the improvement of
them all.

Too humble in its object to attract the attention of sovereigns, the learning apparently unconnected with their policy, was permitted to
pursue its career, undisturbed by the penalties
and terrors of political inquisition. ARISTOTLE
would never have been the favorite of ALEXAN-
DER, if the latter had perceived that philosophy
was destined to become the destroyer of despotism : nor would the revival of letters have been
permitted in Europe, if its monarchs could have
foreseen the consequent abridgment, and perhaps the total subversion of their authority.

* This thought is beautifully enforced in the oration of Cicero pro
Archias.

A latitude of investigation into those sciences, apparently neutral to government, has been the powerful cause of their constant improvement and progression ; every doctrine they maintained, and every proposition they suggested, have been successively submitted to the touchstone of examination. The contact of opposite opinions has annihilated former errors, and led to the discovery of important truths. Experiment by her industry in collecting facts, and judgment by her faculty of combining, distributing, and classing those facts, and of deriving conclusions from them all, has opened to our view many invaluable pages of the important volume of truth. Why then should government, like the secrets of the oracle, be confined to the knowledge of the initiated few ? What substantial reason can be assigned, that civil society should stand a solitary exception among her sister sciences, and be rendered the forbidden tree of knowledge, the fruit of which it is sacrilegious to touch ? Are delusion and error the only practicable means of enforcing political order and obedience ? May not all the rational measures of civil

Subject proposed. government, become enforced by a persuasion of their salutary consequences, and from the conviction of an enlightened understanding ? A consideration of this momentous question, will be the topic of the following pages.

CHAPTER II.

On the general right to investigate Political Topics.

Reciprocity of human duties—Theory of civil so-
ciety—Nature of government—Principle of
responsibleness—Fallibility of government.

T HE present subject of discussion, Chap. II. involves a consideration of the following principal questions : Is it the right of society to inves-
tigate with freedom into the affairs of government ? Is society possessed of abilities competent to the formation of a correct and pertinent
opinion upon political measures ? Do individuals possess the right of communicating the result
of their deliberations upon those topics ? And
should any, and what restrictions be imposed
upon the extent and manner of such communi-

CHAP. II. cation ? The reasoning contained in the present and succeeding chapters, shall be employed in the discussion of the first of those enquiries.

The present is, strictly speaking, a question between society and government. It will therefore involve a consideration of the relation in which they are placed with respect to each other, upon the general principles and theory of political institution.

Recipro-
city of
human
duties.
It is an undeniable position, that a continual reciprocity exists between all the human duties. The existence of an obligation on the one hand, necessarily implies the co-existence of a correspondent right on the other. If it is the duty of one individual to perform a certain act, or to abstain from such performance, it is evident, that another must possess a perfect right to such abstinence or performance. When we say it is the duty of civil government to exercise its powers for the protection of the people, that assertion irresistibly implies a correspondent right of the people to demand such protection from the government.

It has already been perceived, that the source of obligation, is to be traced to the mutual relation subsisting between percipient Beings, and that the reciprocal duties between society and government, originate in their social relations.

The existence of mutual obligation, presupposes a mutual right of examining into its nature and extent. Each of the parties between whom such reciprocity exists, must be entitled to investigate at what precise point the line of duty commences, in what direction it leads, and where it terminates ; they must equally possess the means of becoming apprised of what they are bound to perform, and what they are entitled to receive.

The subject is susceptible of further elucidation, from a review of the genuine nature of human society. *Theory of society.* Whatever disagreement may have existed between the various theories that have obtained with respect to the origin of society, there is an universal coincidence of sentiment concerning the objects it is intended to effect. It is perfectly agreed, that the promotion of general happiness is the only legitimate end of its institution. Even the writers in favor of despotism, are far from denying a proposition, of which the truth is so evident ; on the contrary, they attempt to advocate their system upon the refutable ground, that despotism is the species of civil polity most favorable to the permanent happiness of mankind.

It is unnecessary to enter into a detail of the various speculations which fancy has suggested, concerning the original formation of govern-

CHAP. II. ment.   The nature of that institution, and its
connection with civil society, are sufficiently obvious.   Society is not the instrument of government created for the purpose of affording gran-
deur and consequence to the latter.   It was not
instituted in order that LEOPOLD might become
an Emperor, GEORGE a King, or that our present chief magistrate should be inaugurated
President.   Who will assert, that civil society
was established for the ridiculous pageantry of
pouring a stream of consecrated oil upon the
blood-stained brows of a weak and vicious mor-
tal ?   That crimes and murders should become
legalized by the fascinating code of civil institution ?   That the dagger of the sanguinary assas-
sin should be disguised between the venerable
vestments of social power ?   That the moral sentiments and virtues of mankind, justice, humanity, sensibility, and compassion, should be lost
amidst the dazzling pride and splendor of ambition ?   That every rational perception of the mind,
and all the benevolent emotions of the heart,
should be destroyed by the constant habitude of
desolation, and every varied spectacle of massa-
cre and horror ?

> " Could great men thunder
> As Jove himself does.   Jove would ne'er be quiet,
> For every pelting, petty officer
> Would use his heaven for thunder; nothing but
>   thunder.
> Merciful heaven !

Thou rather with thy sharp and sulphurous bolt
Split'st the unwedgeable and gnarled oak
Than the soft myrtle: O, but man! proud man!
(Drest in a little brief authority;
Most ignorant of what he's most assur'd
His glassy essence) like an angry ape,
Plays such fantastic tricks before high heaven,
As make the angels weep."

SHAKESPEARE.

Whatever speculations may be indulged upon this topic, we must be compelled to consider society as the antecedent, and government
as its necessary consequence.   Government is,
strictly speaking, the creature of society origin-
ating in its discretion, and dependent upon its
will ; with whatever awful habiliments the civil magistrate may be invested—whatever imposing appellations he may assume.   Suppose
him seated on the throne of Eastern pageantry
and splendor—crown'd with the imperial dia-
dem—decorated with purple robes—and armed
with the sceptre of absolute authority—he is habituated to the exercise of unlimited power—
courted by flatterers, idolized by sycophants,
and surrounded by mercenary slaves.   But lo !
a whisper is heard among the multitude, mysterious and portentive.   Like DYONISIUS, the
tyrant trembles on his throne.   Behold the eventful crisis has arrived !—the sovereign voice of
public opinion has declared, that Liberty should
become established.   In an instant the fairy
spell of delusion is dissipated——the tremendous

CHAP. II. authority of this august and magnanimous despot, like the enchanted castle of the magician, vanishes for ever.

With relation to government, public opinion is omnipotent. It is the general will or acquiescence that supports every species of political institution, or rather, to speak more correctly, it is impossible that any government should exist in direct contravention of the general will. Considered in this light, the position is universal in its extent. It is true at Petersburgh and Constantinople, as well as at Philadelphia. The governments of Turkey and Russia, maintain their authority rather in consequence of the public acquiescence, than by virtue of any distinct and previous decision of the national will. The government of the United States is the genuine offspring of a pre-existing determination of public volition. Let us suppose for a moment, that a train of circumstances was to take place in Russia or in Turkey, calculated to convince the people of those countries, that the existence of their respective governments was in diametrical opposition to their happiness and interests, what would be the immediate result of such conviction ? Could the armies of PAUL or of ACHMET withstand the universal will of the inhabitants of their respective empires ? But this proposition would imply, that the conviction and consequent volition of the soldiery, were in unison

with those of their fellow-subjects. In this case
a revolution would be inevitable.

With respect to government, therefore, every
thing is dependent upon the public will. The
powers of society are always adequate to the destruction of its political institutions, whenever
such determination is rendered universally prevalent. Unless the public mind becomes enlightened, what principle or what law is possessed of sufficient energy to prevent it from
leading to the most violent acts of outrage and
desperation? When we examine the records of
any age or country, we tremble at the deplora-
ble catastrophes which have ensued from political ignorance and imposture. We perceive
contending factions combating with each other,
for the inglorious purpose of deciding who shall
be the master of their country. With indignation we pursue the mad career of SYLLA and
MARIUS, and trace them through the fields of
dreadful slaughter and proscription. We behold the Prætorian band, a licentious and pam-
pered soldiery, prostituting the prerogatives of
empire to the most venal and abandoned bidder.* At one moment we behold the guilty ty-

* Upon the barbarous murder of PERTINAX by the Prætorian guards,
this mercenary and ungovernable soldiery, openly proclaimed the Empire of the world for sale to the highest bidder. SULPICIANUS and
DIDIUS JULIANUS were the competitors ; the prize was struck off to
the latter. Let it be remembered, that he did not long enjoy the fruits

CHAP. II. rant, bursting asunder all the bonds of nature and consanguinity, imbrue his hands in the common blood of his family.   At another we view him dying by poison or the dagger.   Such, alas! is history.   Its perusal fills our mind with every contending emotion.   Disgusted or appalled by the sad recital of human miseries and crimes, we abandon the affecting volume, or efface its pages with our tears.

What then is the cause of all this complicated calamity ? It is ignorance and the imposture which it nourishes.   It follows, that the only antidote which can be applied, is the progress of information : in every rational theory of society, it should therefore be established as an essential principle, that freedom of investigation is one of the most important rights of a people. It is true to a proverb, that " ignorance is the parent of vice."   Knowledge is therefore a more powerful corrective than coercion.   By enlightening the understanding, you lay the foundation of positive virtue and benefit.   Punishment, when accurately considered, is itself a multiplication of human calamity.   In every view we contemplate the subject, it is equally the solid interest of government and of society, that the

of his shameless ambition.   In sixty-six days after the fatal purchase, he was deposed and slain ; but he has immortalized a name that would otherwise have slumbered in obscurity.

GIBBON.

public mind should become enlightened : for
the progress of knowledge must become an effectual preventative of that violent revolution
and imposture, which so often marks the person
of the magistrate for its death-devoted victim.

Let us for a moment examine into the nature
of civil government.   What is its genuine province, and from what source does it derive its
powers ?   It is to be observed, that the general
superintendance of government, is rather of a
negative than a *positive* kind.   Its injunctions
are, to abstain from the perpetration of vice, and
not to perform particular acts of virtue.   On the
one side, we are bound to avoid the commission of evil ; and it is within the power of government to reach us by a general prohibition.
But on the score of virtue, there are degrees of
preferableness between one action and another,
too subtle to be embraced by any form of civil
legislation.   Here then we must be left at perfect freedom to decide, independent of the controul of human power.

It is further to be observed, that all human
legislation is circumscribed within very narrow
bounds.   In the language of lawyers, it is rather declaratory than enacting or original.   It
is not within the authority of government to destroy the essential qualities of human action.   It
cannot remove the eternal barrier that separates

CHAP. II. virtue from vice.   When it declares an action
to be criminal, it is either because it violates
the pre-existing laws of morality, or because its
consequences are injurious to society.   But by
what unheard-of arguments can it be maintained, that the exercise of the rational faculties is
criminal or prejudicial to the general welfare ?
Until this extraordinary position is established,
no human legislature can deny our right to the
most unbounded latitude of investigation.

From whence then does government derive
its authority ?   Where are the former reasoners
in favor of *jure divino* power ? Long have they
been laid into the dark and silent tomb, and
their volumes have mouldered into oblivion.   It
cannot be denied, that the powers of government are not original, but strictly derivative ;
that the only fountain from whence its authority
proceeds, is public delegation.   For whatever
may be the particular form of national institution, its existence is equally owing to the general will.   It must ever remain the inherent and
incontrovertible right of society, to dissolve its
political constitution, whenever the voice of public opinion has declared such dissolution to be
essential to the general welfare.   Society must,
therefore, necessarily possess the unlimited right
to examine and investigate.   If government is
the instrument which they adopted for the promotion of general good ; if it is the creature

which they invested with powers for effecting the benevolent design of social felicity ; it is so- ciety that must determine, whether those pur- poses have been realized, or how far they have been departed from. It follows, therefore, as a necessary consequence, that the government which attempts to coerce the progress of opi- nion, or to abolish the freedom of investigation into political affairs, materially violates the most essential principles of the social state.

An important consideration, evidently dedu- cible from the preceding observations, is the re- *Principle of respon- sibleness.* sponsibleness of governments. The principle of responsibleness is universal in its application, and equally extends to every species of political institution : for, in the sight of reason and jus- tice, the most despotic and absolute sovereign, is as amenable to the community, as the limited magistrate of a representative commonwealth. It is plain, that the idea of responsibleness would amount to an egregious absurdity, unless it irresistibly implied a correspondent right of investigation.

It is moreover of importance to enquire, whether government itself is exempted from the *Fallibility of govern- ment.* frailties and imperfections of humanity ? When did infallibility become a distinguished attribute of the human legislator ? At what happy æra were sovereigns and magistrates released from

CHAP. II. the prejudices, errors, and passions that are incident to their fellow-mortals? When did ambition cease to be the lust of Princes, and the extension of prerogative an appetite even of the rulers of the free? Have nations never suffered from the wounds inflicted by their tyrants, or societies become the victims of usurpation, which resulted from ignorance and fatal security? Who, alas! is aware in how eminent a degree the vices and crimes of the multitude, are attributable to the abuses and corruption of political institution? Shall it then be said, that the ages which are to come, must derive no friendly lesson from the experience of those that have passed? Shall no corrective be administered to the follies and wretchedness of society? Knowledge is the only guardian which can prevent us from becoming the vassals of tyranny and the dupes of imposture. Investigation is dangerous to the systems which are founded in despotism and corruption, but it confers additional energy on those that are established upon the genuine foundation of truth. Unless it can be maintained, that despotism is the natural element of social existence, the position must be conceded, that freedom of political enquiry is necessary to the intellectual vigour and sanitude of the human species.

CHAPTER III.

THE SUBJECT CONTINUED.

*Theory of mind—Philosophy of human conduct
—Of the passions—Knowledge their only corrective—Recapitulation—Society the parent of
the sciences.*

THE perfect right of society to investigate political subjects, becomes farther enforced from a consideration of the theory of
mind. By the very constitution of his nature,
man is an intelligent Being : every object by
which he is surrounded, every principle which
is presented to his understanding, necessarily
become the subjects of his contemplation.
When once reflection commences its career,
who can determine the future extent of its researches ? Who can prescribe the topics it may
venture to investigate, and those it shall be prohibited from examining ?

CHAP.
III.   Mind is the common property of man, and
the capacity of knowledge is the inseparable attribute of mind.   It is the constant prerogative
of intellect to extend its researches into every
subject.   Thought springs spontaneously from
the situation in which we are placed, the events
by which we are affected, and the objects that
are presented to our view.   The succession of
ideas is governed by the laws of necessary and
irresistible causation.   When once the intellectual train commences, its direction is not to be
diverted, its force is not to be subdued ; we are
led from subject to subject, and reflection pursues reflection, with a rapidity and subtlety too
astonishingly great to be grasped by the utmost
vigilance of observation.

To prescribe bounds to the empire of thought,
would of all tasks be the most herculean.   He
who is aware of the intimate connection existing between ideas, and has perceived the astonishing subtlety of intellect : He who has investigated the doctrine of association, and been
taught

> " How thoughts to thoughts are link'd with viewless
>   chains,
> Tribes leading tribes, and trains pursuing trains ;"

will never cease to wonder at the stupid per-
versity of that despotism which would attempt
to direct the operations of the mind.

Why was man constituted an intellectual be- ^{CHAP.} III.
ing ? Why was he furnished with the sublime
attribute of reason ? Was it intended that his
most exalted and distinguished powers, should
be chained into a state of dormant quiescence
and inactivity ? Shall it be contended, that his
mental endowments are an useless abortion of
heaven ? If the capacity of knowledge is our
pre-eminent characteristic, why should we be
debarred from investigating those topics which
are most immediately connected with our interest and happiness ?

Most undoubtedly, the percipient as well as
the physical faculties of every being, were bestowed for the benevolent purposes of preservation and felicity. There is no natural right more
perfect or more absolute, than that of investigating every subject which concerns us. The
influence of government and laws is omnipresent, and continually pursues us through every
walk of life. It is not the blind impetuosity of
chance ; it is not the atmosphere or climate, the
direction of the winds, or the rising and sink-
ing of the mercury in the thermometer, that renders us precisely what we are. It is the force
of social institution that forms our manners, and
consequently shapes our disposition, and governs our conduct. Is it not, therefore, of the
greatest importance, that a cause so powerful,

CHAP.
III.
incessant, and universal in its operation, should
be thoroughly investigated and understood?
The exercise of our faculties with respect to
such interesting concern, is a right inseparably
attached to our nature, and which cannot be
subverted without destroying the fundamental
laws of our moral and intellectual constitution.

All knowledge is connected by the most in-
dissoluble ties. One truth will infallibly lead to
the discovery of another, and the laws of percipient causation, will inevitably operate in perpetual geometrical progression. There are only
two alternatives, therefore, presented to the tyrant; he must either endeavour to maintain a
state of gloomy ignorance and barbarism, or tolerate the most unbounded liberty of enquiry.
In vain shall he say to his subjects, " Ye may
explore the extensive fields of nature. Ye may
investigate the abstract truths of science ; but
remember, there stands a forbidden tree in the
gardens of philosophy. I have enshrouded it
with an impenetrable cloud of darkness. I
have fortified it with the palisades of criminal
jurisprudence. Beware! approach not the sacred sanctuary of prerogative, nor touch the
mysterious institutions of my empire." Such
interdiction would be the offspring of a fatal ignorance of the eternal principles of mind. A
general proficiency in knowledge, would infallibly lead to a discovery of the legitimate theory

of government : the flimsy artifices which had covered the crimes of imposture, would no longer disguise their enormity, nor protect them from the indignation of popular justice. Truth would penetrate into the luxury of the palace, and dart her illuminations into the horrors of the dungeon. The intellectual powers are incessant and indefatigable in their operation, and when once they have commenced their task, their labours can never be suspended.

But why should civil government be concealed within the sable mantle of obscurity ? What rational principle can be assigned to induce us to believe, that the mysteries of State should be hidden from vulgar examination ? The general truths of morality, are the subjects of constant investigation. By what chain of reasoning shall we prove the impropriety of political discussion? Is it the interest of society to remain ignorant of its wrongs, or is it the prerogative of government that its abuses should be kept secret ? If it is contended, that political investigation is dangerous to the existence of despotism, and that the safety of a tyrant depends upon the ignorance of the people ; should it be objected, that the extension of knowledge will infallibly lead to the detection of error and to the correction of abuses, these positions will be cheerfully admitted : political reformation will be the inevitable result of the freedom of enquiry—in-

vestigation will become the powerful benefactor of society, and the inflexible enemy of imposture.

The government which is founded upon the
adamant of truth, has nothing to fear from the
progress of political discussion.   It is the interest of such government to solicit, instead of
eluding observation.   If patriotism is its attribute, it should rejoice at the friendly approach
of reformation ; it should acknowledge, that
improvement is a salutary law of our nature, and
that every art and science has been rendered
more perfect by the masterly hand of cultivation.   If it is possible, that such a government
should in reality exist, sincerely attached to the
happiness of the people, and disposed to sacrifice
the momentary gratification of personal ambition, to the substantial glory of contributing to
universal happiness ; to that government it
would become a sublime and animating reflection, that political institution and society are
alike susceptible of progressive improvement.
Such a government would sternly prohibit every
unnecessary innovation, but it would impartially examine every principle that tended to political improvement ; it would discountenance the
visionary projector, whose systems are founded
in the idle dreams of speculation, yet patronize
the judicious and skilful architect, whose abili-

ties were competent to the real amendment of
the temple of public felicity.

Were it necessary to multiply the arguments
upon this subject, the preceding observations
might become illustrated and enforced, from a
consideration of the philosophy of human conduct. It must be apparent, upon the slightest
investigation of this topic, that all the social and
relative duties are derivable from principles, of
which the understanding is the percipient : it
follows therefore, as a necessary consequence,
that the method of establishing the existence of
those duties, must be by argument addressed to
the rational faculties.   Let it for a moment be
supposed, that we are placed in the midst of a
popular assembly, and that it is our province or
our inclination, to persuade our auditors to pursue a given course of conduct : let it be imagined, we are desirous they should petition for
the repeal of a particular law, what are the
measures we would naturally adopt? Would we
not endeavour to convince them, that such law
was irrational in its principles, or injurious in its
consequences ? Would we not strive to prove it
to be repugnant to justice, or hostile to the public good ? What then would such conduct evidently imply ? Is not the conclusion obvious,
that we are addressing beings, intelligent like
ourselves, possessed of common feelings, actuated by similar motives, and capable of estimat-

CHAP. ing their actions by the universal standard of
III.
propriety? Who then will deny, that intelligence is the common attribute of mankind, or
assert, that our actions are impelled by an invisible direction, instead of being governed by the
influence of motives that are present to our understanding?

It may indeed be objected, that " men are
Of the
Passions. liable to be misled by the impetuous ebulition
of the passions, and that our conduct is impelled by the excitement of intemperate feelings,
as often as it is governed by the rational decisions of the judgment; that an appeal to the
passions is the common instrument of orators,
and the hackneyed weapon of popular leaders,
whenever they address a mixed and tumultuous
assemblage?" Such objection is deservedly entitled to the most serious attention :—as far as
the consideration operates, it tends to enforce
the necessity of political enquiry.

In discussing the true merits of such objection, it is essentially important, to consider the
meaning of the principal term it employs; and
to settle the precise signification in which it is
to be received.

What are we to understand by the term passion? Are we to conceive it as implying certain
distinctive emotions or operations of the mind,

or denoting something entirely separate from any modification of mental operation ?

The term passion has been employed in various acceptations.* It sometimes signifies propensities arising from physical organization, such as hunger and sexual desire : in this sense it is certainly foreign to the present subject of enquiry. Secondly, it may imply any extraordinary or vehement excitement of the mind. And thirdly, it is used to express certain distinctive impressions or emotions. of mind, such as revenge or anger, ambition or avarice.

But, receiving the term in either of its significations, it is a position universally true, that knowledge is the only preservative against the inordinate excitement of the passions. It is the genuine and incessant operation of judgment, to estimate the consequences of human action, and to decide upon its propriety, from the effects which are probable to result. If the language of the preceding objection, supposes that the multitude are liable to be misled by the irresistible fury of passion, it is because the multitude are less enlightened than the philosopher.

Knowledge their only corrective.

The Areopagus at Athens would not tolerate the language of declamation. It sternly

* Vide Godwin's political justice.

forbad any appeal to be directed to the passions. Should we fancy that a DEMOSTHENES was addressing that august tribunal, we would naturally presume, that he would use a different manner from that which he would employ in addressing a meeting of the people ; that he would sacrifice the fallacious ornaments of rhetoric, to the grave and substantial truths of argument. In what respects did the venerable member of the Areopagus differ from the common citizen of Athens ? Was his nature originally less susceptible of the influence or operation of the passions ? Did any mystic power or any hidden charm, exempt him from the infirmities of humanity? Can any other reason be assigned for his superiority, than because his judgment had been matured and strengthened by the habit of moral and legal disquisition ? Let it be imagined, that the common citizen had been equally accustomed to investigate the truths of morality, that he had been furnished with equal opportunities to improve his intellectual perceptions ; in such case, what difference would have existed between the vulgar Athenian and the enlightened Areopagite ?

The savage is more strongly impelled by the tyranny of the passions, than civilized man ; the latter is more subject to the dominion of intemperate emotions, than the philosopher : superior cultivation of the percipient faculties, is alone

the cause of this otherwise astonishing diversity. CHAP.
III.
Knowledge is the only guardian principle,
which can rescue us from the fatal despotism of
irregular excitement. The extension of science,
is the only rational method of establishing the
universal empire of truth and virtue.

In proportion as the human mind becomes
enlightened and enlarged, our conduct will be
more closely connected with the decisions of
the understanding—we will be taught to form a
proper estimate of the various objects to which
our volition should become directed. Superior
discernment renders us acquainted with the
means which contribute to permanent happiness. We perceive that the objects of irregular
passion, are unsubstantial and delusive ; while
the advantages of virtue are real and universal.
Let it be supposed, that ambition or avarice,
hatred or revenge, intemperance or voluptuous-
ness, are our predominant propensities, which
lead with tyrant power the direction of our actions. It is observable, that such are passions,
usually the most strong and uncontroulable in
their operation. Are they productive of individual benefit or injury ? Can the gratifications
they produce maintain a competition with the
evils they inflict ? Are their allurements equally
irresistible by the peasant and philosopher ?
Do they impel us to a violation of the moral

CHAP. III. and social duties? Do they deprive us of that serene sublimity of feeling, which arises from the consciousness of rectitude? It is to be observed, that the gratification arising from the indulgence of the passions, is momentary and evanescent; while the sting which succeeds it, is poignant and corrosive. The pleasure which originates from the practice of the opposite virtues, is permanent and substantial: health animates the countenance, and tranquility harmonizes the mind. What moralist will deny the necessary connection between virtue and felicity, or that wretchedness is the necessary concomitant of vice?

Judgment is that property of the mind, which recognizes the importance of such propositions. If we frequently err in estimating the real value of our objects of pursuit; if we often indulge in the gratification of momentary propensities, at the expence of future pain and disappointment, it is because we have not sufficiently advanced in the school of knowledge and experience: it is because our minds have not been habituated to the salutary discipline of moral discussion. If the period shall ever arrive, in which it shall become a general practice to investigate the subjects of morality and politics, society will then become enabled to decide with accuracy upon the merits of human action. Every man will partake, in some degree, of the benefit of

such general illumination : reason will become Chap. III.
the universal standard of decision, and the em-
pire of judgment will succeed to the pernicious
dominion of the passions.

In the conduct which proceeds from the im-
pulse of the passions, our volition is less perfect,
than in that which originates from the decisions of
the understanding. The actions impelled by the
operation of passion, greatly partake of the automatic quality : in those which proceed from the
previous determination of judgment, the operation of will is more perfect, distinct, and dis-
cernible. The being who is propelled by the
habitual tempest of the passions, is little superior to that machine, of which the movements
are directed by wind or water, and irresistibly
dependent upon the laws of gravitation.

It will not perhaps be travelling too far into
the regions of speculation, to assert, that in
proportion as we become proficient in knowledge, our conduct will be governed by the regular influence of motive ; the number of our
voluntary actions will receive perpetual accession, while those which are automatic will pro-
portionally decrease. Let the human mind become enlightened ; let reflection extend her researches throughout the unlimited empire of science ; let the judgment possess and exercise
ample means of invigoration : every action of

mankind will then be capable of becoming traced to the pre-existing determinations of understanding. If our perception of obligation becomes more clear and comprehensive, is it not
evident, that such superior correctness of decision, must infallibly produce a proportionate
effect upon our conduct ?

        From the reasonings contained in the prece-
Recapi- ding and present chapters, it must be evident,
tulation. that as man is the constant object of moral and
social duties, and the perpetual subject of political discipline ; it is necessary that he should
possess and exercise, the means of investigating
the nature and extent of such obligation and
discipline.   From a just and accurate review of
the theory of civil society and government, it is
apparent, that political institution is but the instrument of society ; intended to promote its
prosperity and happiness—that the laws of morality are possessed of universal jurisdiction, and
are obligatory upon the prince and the magistrate, as well as upon the obscure and private
individual—that governments partake of human
fallibility and imperfection, and that they are
responsible to the people, for the faithful performance of their important trusts—that intelligence is the common property of human beings, and that the progress of knowledge is the
only practicable method of diminishing the ascendency of vice, and destroying the dominion

of the passions. From all these considerations Chap. III.
it has been maintained, that a liberty of investigation into every subject of thought, is not only the perfect and absolute right of civil society ; but that the unrestricted exercise of that right, is indispensable to the progression and happiness of mankind. It follows, therefore, that the government which attempts to impede the universal dissemination of science, or to restrain the unlimited career of intellect, may be classed among the most inveterate enemies of the human species.

Previous to dismissing the present branch of our enquiry, let it be remarked, that the cultivation of intellect, and the progress of literature, may be ranked among the foremost benefits derived from society : for, independent of the social state, what would have been the boasted faculties, and where the astonishing inventions of mankind ? Where should we have sought for the arts, or how discovered the numerous truths of science ? Refinement and knowledge, have been the offspring of civilized life ; the solitary man would scarcely be recognized as a moral or intellectual Being : deprived of the advantages of intercourse, he would be unpossessed of language, that happy instrument so necessary in the operations of the mind, and so essential to the communication of our thoughts. It is society that has laid the foundation of know-

Society the parent of the sciences.

_{CHAP.}
_{III.} ledge ; it has furnished all the means of improv-
ing the human faculties, and of perpetuating
those improvements ; it has recorded the discoveries of former ages for the lasting benefit of
succeeding generations ; it has taught us the use
of language and of letters ; it has united the
powers of individual intellect into a common
bank, and multiplied the *peculium* of each by a
general combination of the whole.   The government that interferes with the progress of
opinion, subverts the essential order of the social state.

Let political institution be confined to its genuine objects of superintendance ; let its powers be exclusively directed to the suppression of
crime ; let us say to government, " You have
no legitimate empire over opinion. You have no
equitable jurisdiction over the operations of the
mind : let science explore the unlimited regions
of contemplation.   Truth and virtue are the only
objects of her pursuit.   If your dominion is established in justice, you have nothing to apprehend.
Tyranny alone should tremble at the sternly inquisitive glance of enlightened investigation.   Improvement is an universal law of human nature.
Legislation in common with every other subject
of meditation, must finally submit to its amelio-
rating influence."

CHAPTER IV.

On the competency of Society to investigate Political Topics.

The question proposed—Similarity of human ta-
lents—Philosopher and peasant contrasted—
Theories respecting the diversity of talents—
Attempted to be reconciled—Philosopher and
peasant compared—Of the moral sense—Go-
vernment no monopolist of wisdom—Human
faculties improvable—General capacity of dis-
tinguishing between virtue and vice.

A RE communities, in general, competent to decide upon the propriety of the measures of government? There is no question
which involves considerations of more extensive
magnitude to human society than the present ;
because it will probably become manifest, that
the security, and even the importance of civil
liberty, essentially depend upon an affirmative
decision.—The reasoning of the preceding chap-

ters, has been principally employed to enforce the perfect *right* of society to the exercise of political discussion : but if our decision should terminate in the negative of the preceding question, in vain would the most powerful arguments establish the perfect right of investigation ; in vain would we contend for the existence of a privilege that was useless and incapable of active exertion.   Little would be gained by a most decisive victory in the argument, unless it should be equally evident, that *abilities* may reside in society, adequate to the formation of a correct and pertinent opinion.

In the examination of this question, the first consideration which naturally becomes presented, is the striking uniformity that exists in the human understanding.   Intelligence is the common attribute of man.   The science in which one individual is capable of becoming proficient, is in general open to the attainment of another. Knowledge is not a rare and uncommon gem which a few are destined to monopolize :   on the contrary, its treasures are susceptible of universal communication.

Truth, as an abstract term, is altogether insusceptible of definition.   The most sagacious reasoner has hitherto been unable by any circumlocution or form of phraseology, to describe with accuracy in what its essence consists.   But whatever may be the abstract nature of truth, its evidences are capable of equal presentation to the percipient powers of all men. It is not a courtier whose residence is confined to palaces, nor is it always to be found in the solemn gravity of a deliberative assembly. Whether it relates to principles or facts, it is to be discovered and ascertained by judgment ; and judgment is a faculty possessed in common by mankind.

It is true, that the picture of society presents a great variety of talent ; but still the resemblance is much more striking than the dissimilarity. The diversity we perceive, is principally owing to the habits we imbibe, the education we receive, and the opportunities with which we are furnished. Contrast Sir ISAAC NEWTON with the common husbandman or labourer ; how immense is the disparity between them ! Can we doubt that the superior learning and illumination of the sage, is principally derived from the influence of cultivation ?

Let us pay a visit to the philosopher in his cradle, and afterwards attend to the lispings of the infant peasant. We find that their organs of sensation are similar. Whatever contributes to the pain or pleasure of the one, produces precisely the same effect upon the other. Pre-

sently the period of adolescence commences.
The young Sir Is aac is presented with the clas-
sics, and the stores of Grecian and Roman learning are unfolded to his expanding view. He is
furnished with learned tutors to direct his studies and pursuits, and receives the rudiments of
scholastic education within the walls of an university. The current of his thought is extended
throughout the varied fields of literature and
refinement.   His attention becomes directed
to the acquisition of science. He corresponds
and associates with the most enlightened ornaments of his age ; profits by their information, and receives the benefit of their discoveries.   By habitually contemplating the laws of
nature, his perceptions become corrected, and
his understanding is rendered profound.   It is
natural that we should imbibe a strong attachment to our favorite objects of pursuit : hence
the emulation of superior excellence, and a thirst
for literary glory, are predominant incentives in
the bosom of the philosopher : for these he trims
the midnight lamp, and travels through the let-
tered lore.

From surveying the progress of the accomplished sage, let us return to the humble in-
mate of the cottage. How few in comparison
are the means of knowledge presented to his
view ! In the day his youthful hands are enured
to labour ; in the evening he beholds the gyra-

tions of the busy spinning-wheel : his life is Chap. IV.
spent in the uniformity of insipid though
useful pursuit.   It may be that some little vil-
lage school has imparted to him its slender pit-
tance of rustic learning, or perhaps the worthy
parish clergyman has condescended to unfold
to him some solitary truths of religion or morality.   What an immeasurable distance exists between the opportunities furnished to the philosopher and the husbandman ! Is it certain, that
the juvenile Newton exhibited any astonishing indication of future brilliancy and talents ?
If he had exchanged situations with the unlet-
tered rustic, who will venture to pronounce,
that the latter might not have become his equal
in scientific excellence and fame ? Who will assert, that the inequality of education is insuffi-
cient to produce such disparity of intellectual attainment ?*

There are few controversies in which the op- Theories respecting the diversity of talent.
posite reasoners have exhibited more pertinaci-
ty of opinion, than in that which relates to
the causes of diversity in talents.   On the
one side it has been strenuously contended, that
the difference which we constantly discover in
the abilities of men, is principally owing to the Original inequality
original soil or stamina of mind ; and that it is

---

* Newton himself, with modesty truly honorable, and perhaps with
much truth, attributed his own acquirements to application.   In a letter
to Dr. Bentley, he declared, " that if he had done the world any service,
it was due to nothing but industry and patient thought.

CHAP.
IV. the necessary result of the varieties of physical structure. It is asserted, that the organs of sensation in one man, are more exquisite than those of another ; and that therefore his feelings and perceptions will be rendered proportionably accurate and acute. It is also maintained, that some individuals naturally possess a peculiar genius or aptitude, for excelling in a particular art or pursuit ; that CICERO was born an orator, and HOMER a poet ; and that however education may have unfolded and enlarged their powers, the embrio of peculiar excellence must always have been in their possession.

Education and habit. On the other side it is contended, that every thing is the result of education and habit ; that mind is of too subtle and delicate a nature, to become materially affected by the gross operation of physical causes ; that the diversity of genius may arise from the force and bias of early and even antenatal impression ; but that it does not exist in the original stamina of mind.

Attempted to be reconciled The solution of this difficult problem, is by no means essential to the general purposes of our present enquiry. It involves considerations so abstruse, as to foil and bewilder the utmost vigilance of attention. Perhaps each of these contending systems, may in some measure be founded in truth. It is probable, that they may justly become reconciled, by allowing each of

those causes to possess a proper degree of operation. But whatever diversity may exist in the
original genius and talents of mankind, it must
be constrained to yield to the superior powers
of habit and education. Knowledge is not in-
tuitive, however extraordinary may have been
their respective talents. Without cultivation,
TULLY would not have been an orator; NEW-
TON could not have explored the laws of the
universe ; nor would HOMER have stood unrivalled in the career of epic poetry.

However great may be the diversity in human genius and talents, in the subjects of moral
disquisition, there is but little inequality. With
respect to those subjects, there exists a perfect
uniformity in feeling and in sentiment. The laws
of morality are correspondent at Paris and Hin-
dostan, and the standard of decision is the common property of mankind.

Place NEWTON and the peasant in an inter-   Philoso-
esting point of view : they are joint spectators   pher and
peasant,
of a melancholy scene ; they behold a ruffian   compared
seize the fatal dagger, and plunge it in the bosom of an unoffending victim ! Will the philosopher become agitated with the united emotions of pity, horror, and indignation ? And
will not the feelings of his humble companion
be parallel with his own ?—Inform the philosopher of the sudden death of a favorite child, and

instantly you rend his soul with grief. Tell the unhappy husbandman that his beloved wife and offspring are no more, will not his anguish be as poignant as that of the sage? Again, let us suppose that the man of refinement and the peasant are in company, and that they behold a wretched victim immolated on the scaffold; presently they are told, that his judge or his executioner in reality committed the crime for which he innocently bleeds; will not the philosopher shudder at the injustice of the sentence? And will his illiterate attendant be less forcibly affected by its enormity?

Of the
moral
sense.
There is abundant evidence to prove, that all men are possessed of what is termed the MORAL SENSE. It matters little in the argument, whether such common property be innate or acquired. Our perceptions concerning the nature of moral and social obligation, are entirely similar, and our decisions with respect to them, will in general be uniform and correspondent.

Even admitting the inequality and extensive variety of human *genius*, it is nevertheless evident, that the attribute of *judgment* is more generally and impartially distributed. It is the property of genius* to invent and execute; it is the province of judgment to discriminate and

* Blair's lectures.

decide. The investigation of moral or political
subjects, requires not the talent of invention;
judgment and not genius is the faculty to be
employed. The true merits of the present enquiry will be comprised in the proposition, that the
medium of human capacity, is competent to decide upon the ordinary detail of politics.

Whatever can be performed by one man, can
in general be accomplished by another. With
equal application we are capable of equal attainments. The extraordinary powers of a few
distinguished individuals, may constitute exceptions to the general rule, but they cannot otherwise destroy the universality of its application.

Moreover, it can never be contended, that Govern-
it is the property of government to monopolize ment no monopo-
the wisdom of society. We will suppose, that list of wisdom.
it is directed by three hundred persons, in their
different stations or official gradations. The
nation consists of many millions. If we consider the origin of government, or for want
of better data, apply the doctrine of chances;
the probability will be, that many thousands
exist in the community, superior in discernment
and erudition, to those concerned in administration. Is it not of all absurdities the most incon-
gruous, that government should dictate perpetual silence and torpor to those who excel in intellect? On the other hand, can it exercise a

CHAP.
IV.
more atrocious despotism, than to debar those who are inferior in intelligence, from that intellectual improvement, which is the characteristic of our species? Let the fortunate individuals, in whom the chapter of circumstances has placed the affairs of state, be contented with the exercise of that legitimate power, which is sanctioned by reason and the civil constitution : it would be the excess of wanton inhumanity, to put a termination to the career of human intellect.

But yesterday, the exalted individuals who fill the most elevated stations, and possess the most powerful offices in the state, were promoted from a private rank and station in society. What sudden exertion of magical energy has in an instant illuminated their minds, with wisdom beyond the comprehension of the ordinary race of mortals? When did it become a property of government, in any eminent degree, to multiply or enlarge the intellectual qualifications of its administrators? When was it known, that the possession of civil authority in any perceptible shape, embellished the mind, or invigorated the understanding.

The exercise of reason is appurtenant to man in his individual capacity. In the humble walks of private life, we may search for wisdom, and discover every virtue. Philosophy, the most re-

fined, abilities the most cultivated, and scienti- _{CHAP.}
fic attainments the most highly finished, are not IV.
unfrequently to be found in a garret.   In the
lowliest stations and amidst the obscurest paths,
the choicest germs of intellect are often doomed
to wither and to languish unnoticed and unknown.   The most exalted heroism, and the
most extensive talents, are frequently destined
to slumber in eternal obscurity.

> " Full many a gem of purest ray serene,
> The dark unfathom'd caves of ocean bear ;
> Full many a flow'r is born to blush unseen,
> And waste its sweetness on the desart air.
>
> Some village HAMPDEN, that, with dauntless breast,
> The little tyrant of his fields withstood ;
> Some mute inglorious MILTON, here may rest ;
> Some CROMWELL, guiltless of his country's blood."
>   GRAY.

Still it is to be observed, that the interference
of government, is by no means favorable to the
progression of literature : it is only the inob-
trusive petition of science, that no insalutary
coercion should be exercised to impede its progress, or present an obstacle to its career.

We might hazard the decision of this subject,
upon the solidity of the following propositions :
first, that the faculties of all men are susceptible of continual improvement : and secondly,

Chap.
IV.

that all men are possessed of the means of distinguishing virtue from vice, benefits from injuries, and justice from its opposite.—Unless the
human capacity was susceptible of improvement,
the arts and the sciences would be useless to the
world. Indeed from the reverse of this proposition, it would infallibly follow, that no such thing
as science could ever have existed. Ignorance
must have preceded information, and the progress of mind must of necessity have commenced, from the most trivial and imperceptible be-
ginnings. Unless the knowledge of one was
communicable to another, the office of the preceptor would be wholly unserviceable, and the
discoveries of wisdom unprofitable and nugato-
ry. If education can form the lawyer, mathe-
matician, and divine, why cannot attention and
application, render us proficient in political
knowledge ?

Human faculties improvable.

To discriminate between virtue and vice,
forms an essential proportion of the education of
every intellectual Being. Human life necessarily produces an unceasing series of perceptions,
opinions, and actions ; it may be considered as
a state of incessant, moral, and political discipline. It is the perpetual destiny of man to become tutored in the school of experience ; the
numerous relations in which we are placed with
respect to others ; the various spheres in which
we are called upon to suffer and to act, neces-

All men capable of distin-guishing between virtue and vice.

sarily unfold the nature, and impress the importance of obligation.   The discernment of evil
commences at a very early period of existence ;
the juvenile culprit will shrink from observation ;
his faultering tongue, and palsied limbs, be-
speak emotions arising from the internal conviction of offence.   How soon do we learn to blush
at falsehood ! How early will the crimson glow
upon our cheeks betray the consciousness of
guilt ; while at the welcome sound of praise,
our youthful eyes will sparkle with the honest
satisfaction of rectitude.

It is the prerogative of justice, to dart its illuminations into every mind.   Wherever man
exists, the laws of morality will establish their
immutable empire.   It is the inseparable attribute of an intelligent Being, to perceive the nature and character of human conduct, upon
whatever theatre it is displayed : he can readily
discover the path of rectitude in the walks of
common life ; nor does it require miraculous in-
spiration, to penetrate the general spirit and
tendency of political institution.

Justice is a standard of universal authority ;
it is equally applicable to the conduct of individuals and of nations. Governments as well as
men, are the subjects of moral and social obligation : they are equally bound to abstain from
oppression and injuries ; their acts of injustice

CHAP.
IV.
and tyranny, are as marked and distinguishable as the vices of private life, and their errors are equally exposed to the light of observation.

Whatever constitutes despotism or cruelty, will be continually the same. Considerations of rank and power, can never alter the genuine character of human action : if the scymeter is stained with innocent blood, it matters nothing whether the fatal blow was struck by a monarch or a robber. Oppression and crime are the same in every quarter of the globe ; the experience of mankind, with respect to their characteristics, will be constant and uniform ; upon those subjects, therefore, the sentence of the human understanding, will be ever steady and correspondent.

He who can form a proper estimate of individual conduct and morality, will be also enabled to form a tolerably correct opinion of the measures and morality of the cabinet. By the frequent habits of discussion, his discriminating powers will be rendered more acute, and his decisions will improve in accuracy ; upon most questions his judgment will be competent to distinguish ; the principal requisite will be to furnish him with the necessary means of information, and to present the case with copiousness and perspicuity to his view.

CHAPTER V.

THE SUBJECT CONTINUED.

*Enquiry respecting government——Government
founded in morals——An objection——Answered
——Judgment, a common attribute——Distinct
from genius——Nature of political subjects——
Private and public morality——Identical——Application.*

LET us now proceed, and enquire
into the nature of that institution, which is generally known by the name of civil government.
There is no exercise that can be more important, or more closely connected with the principal subject of discussion, than an examination
of the genuine principles, which enter into the
foundation of political institution. We have
perceived, that *man,* from the essential constitution of his nature, is a moral and intelligent
Being : and that a knowledge of the principles

Chap. of morality, is inseparable from his natural and
V. social existence. If therefore, it should be
found on such examination, that political institution, is established upon those universal principles of *ethics*, which are the common property
of mankind, the conclusion will be inevitable,
that they are qualified to investigate the nature,
and to decide upon the merits of political subjects.

Govern-   Government, by which is understood the ad-
ment
founded in ministration of public affairs, is not a mysterious
morals. system, involved in impenetrable obscurity, nor
is it a science attended with inexplicable difficulty. In theory, it is established upon principles of universal application, and founded in
maxims, which are readily embraced, and comprehended by the most common understanding.
The laws of morality are open to all men ; they
are comprised in a volume, which all may read,
and all may comprehend. It is undeniable,
that the foundation of civil government, is to
be discovered in the extensive science of
morals.

The practical detail of government, is a series
of decisions and measures, in affirmance of the
principles established in its theory. To pronounce with accuracy upon any given act of
administration—to discover the merits or the
impolicy of any particular statute—to perceive

its consonancy or disagreement with the general principles of justice—to decide how far the practice, is in perfect unison with the theory of government, requires only the exercise of that judgment, which is the common attribute of humanity, combined with such information, as every intelligent Being can with application acquire.

It may indeed be tauntingly objected, " that Objection. men are not born politicians or philosophers; neither are they constitutionally metaphysicians or divines." Shall the most abstruse questions in philosophy, be submitted to the examination of the illiterate and the uncultivated? Shall the most complicated and difficult investigations of science, be referred to the rude and unhallowed inspection of vulgar minds? Has not every profession, and every occupation in common life, secrets peculiar to itself, difficulties, which can only become vanquished by unremitted labour and assiduity? Shall it be affirmed, that every man possesses competent penetration, to explore the depths, and trace the diversified windings of civil polity?

To this it may be answered, that every intel- Answer. lectual Being is possessed of the attribute of judgment; and that the common medium of such discriminating faculty, is abundantly sufficient to decide, upon the customary detail of

CHAP.
V. human affairs. Politics, is neither poetry, spe-
culative philosophy, metaphysics, or polemic
theology. To investigate the merits of a poem,
requires that degree of critical erudition, which
can only proceed from arduous habitude of
study, and profound acquaintance with what is
generally denominated polite literature.—To
imitate the epic strains of the Iliad, the Aenead,
or Paradise Lost, presupposes the possession
of an extraordinary faculty, in addition to *judgment*, usually expressed by the appellation *genius*. *Judgment*, by which is meant the power
of comparing, reflecting, and deciding, is a
species of common property, distributed in a
more equal and impartial degree, among the
whole percipient creation. *Genius* is a qualification more diversified in its nature, and more
rarely bestowed ; the wild career of fancy, the
bold, adventurous, and exploring flight of imagination ;—she is to be found in the lively sallies
of the orator, and discovered in the sublime
imagery of the poet.—Disdaining every species
of subjugation, she claims an independence of
the sovereign empire of truth ;—she sallies into
the visionary abodes of fiction, and darts with
lightning speed, into the grotesque regions of
invention and romance.—Not contented with
the realities of the moral and physical world,
she forms new creations of her own, annexes
eagle's wings to men, and attributes human
speech to eagles ; she tortures nature with her

Judgment
a common
attribute.

Distinct
from ge-
nius.

vagaries, and distorts it with her gambols.   By _{Chap.}
turns, she forms an angel, and moulds a Cali- ^{V.}
ban.   Like herself, her language is eccentric,
original, peculiar, and characteristic.   That of
judgment is solid, perspicuous, and convincing.
It is the power of genius to execute and invent:
it is the property of judgment to examine and
decide.   The essence of genius is to ornament,
amuse, and embellish : the character of judgment is permanent utility.   If every individual
has not the distinguished and brilliant gift of
genius, he at least possesses an inestimable portion of the more substantial attribute of judgment.

Neither genius, nor exquisite subtlety of refinement, is necessary to the ordinary disquisition of politics.   Poetry is an intellectual ornament ; its object is rather to embellish and
amuse, than to enlighten and instruct.   Metaphysics and polemics abound in obscurity, they
are fraught with incertitude, and pregnant with
inexplicable mysticism.   Many who have been
most profoundly conversant with the subtleties
of THOMAS AQUINAS, or the laborious researches of a BENTLEY, or MALBRANCHE,
have been constrained to lament the sacrifice of
time, in frivolous and unsatisfactory pursuits.

Such are the studies which elude the utmost
profundity of intellect ; they lead us into the

CHAP.
V.
world of shadows and invisibilities, where nothing can be distinctly perceived; because every
object (if objects they are) is enveloped with the
atmosphere of obscurity. The existences of
that world, are too highly subtilized and atte-
nuated, to be brought into contact with our
senses; they are wholly imperceptible to the
keenest eye; they baffle the vigilance of the
most sublimated understanding; we are furnished with no substantial data from which to
reason; experience instead of invigorating the
mind, only serves to convince us of the futility
of our researches.

Not so with rational politics. Every truth is
luminous; every principle is clear, perspicuous,
and determinable; its doctrines are established
in the common sentiments and feelings of mankind; its positions are maintained and enforced
by universal experience. Whatever relates to
human duty, is susceptible of demonstrative
certainty. The language of justice is uniformly
legible; its characters are written by omnipotent wisdom, upon the tablets of our hearts.

Nature
of politi-
cal sub-
jects.

The morality of common life, concerns the
social and relative duties, arising from the reciprocal intercourse of man. Those duties must
be of universal perception, because they are
possessed of universal obligation. It would be
absurd and tyrannical, to constrain a rational

Private
morality.

being to the performance of conduct, with the CHAP.
V.
reasons and principles of which, he is destined
to remain entirely unacquainted.

The morality which regulates the intercourse Public
morality.
of sovereigns, is identical with that which go-
verns the conduct of individuals. It is not barely the verisimilitude of the former, but the very
same principle operating upon a more extended
theatre. Justice is essentially the same, whe- Identical.
ther applied to private individuals or to sovereign States ; the cases are not only similitu-
dinary, they are strictly and perfectly identical.

What is the idea annexed to the term nation?
Does it not constantly designate an aggregation
or multitude of individuals ? Men are the constituent unities which enter into the composition of society. Man, therefore, is the only actor
upon whatever theatre human conduct is destined to become exhibited. To whatever object
our imagination is extended, to the statesman
in the cabinet, the philosopher in his closet, or
the hero in the field ; wherever we direct our
contemplation to battles, and to sieges, nego-
tiations or hostility, to treaties of peace, convention of commerce, or declarations of war; it
is *man* that acts and suffers. We still perceive
his character ; we read his virtues and his vices,
discover his passions and propensities, unmask
his follies, detect his errors, and decide upon

CHAP.
V.
his actions, by the universal standard of morality.

He that possesses an adequate perception of
individual obligation and morality, must consequently possess a perspicuous acquaintance with
the duties enforced by the morality of nations.
It is not indeed asserted, that the perception of
justice is innate or instinctive. Without resorting to such controvertible hypothesis, it is sufficient to contend, that no social Being can be
ignorant of its principles ; because they are necessarily derived from that experience and education, which is the result of his intercourse
with society.

Appli-
cation.
To apply these observations more immediately to the question, it is evident, that man as a
moral Being, and the constant object of moral
and social discipline, must, from his necessary
experience and habits, possess a considerable
knowledge of the principles of moral law. It is
also sufficiently plain, that the duties attached
to the intercourse of nations and individuals, arise
from the identical fountain of obligation, and
must therefore be in a great measure familiar to
every understanding.—Without possessing extraordinary depth of intellect, we can readily
perceive, whether any given action will be de-
trimental to our neighbour. We can as readily
discern those actions which terminate in public

injury : indeed most offences pronounced of a
public nature, consist of injuries primarily inflicted upon individuals, and which considerations of general policy, have rendered a common
cause.—Without pretensions to superior discernment, every person can as easily perceive what
conduct in one nation violates the rights, and
operates to the detriment of another ; or what
acts of a government infallibly terminate in personal injury and oppression. Hence then it is
an obvious position, that every intelligent Being
must necessarily possess a sufficient standard of
political discrimination.

Can the obstinacy of scepticism demand still
farther illustration ? Does so evident a proposition require additional argument ? Judgment is
the common property of intellectual Beings, and
justice is the moral element with which it is
principally conversant. We have seen that the
jurisdiction of equity, equally embraces the subjects of national and individual concern : the
question is, however, susceptible of still stronger
elucidation, from a more particular examination into the nature and genuine operation of civil government.

CHAPTER VI.

THE SUBJECT CONTINUED.

W E are now to take a more intimate survey of government, in the various attitudes in which it is usually presented. We are to contemplate its ordinary detail of administration ; to consider its operations, domestic and

CHAP.
VI. foreign, in peace and in war ; and to investigate the principles by which its transactions are
or should be regulated.

We have seen that man is the constant subject of moral and social obligation—that the natural and civil relations in which he is placed,
constitute the foundation of a perpetual system
of duties ; but his passions, his habits, his wants,
and his imperfect state of being, expose him to
continual temptations or inducements to swerve
from the path of rectitude.   Hence the necessity of introducing a superintending jurisdiction :
this general superintendant is government.

What then is the genuine and rational province of that institution, usually expressed by
the term government ? Notwithstanding the various subtleties, and multitude of refinements in
which the subject has been enveloped, perhaps
the whole legitimate operation of political establishment, is strictly reducible to two simple
heads.   First, its general superintendance over
the internal affairs of society ; and secondly, its
protective energy against the aggression and
hostility of foreign states.

I. Inter-
nal regu-
lation.   In the first of these branches, consists its interference in the prevention of offences, and its
employment of coercion for the reparation of injuries, and for the purposes of example and

prevention—not from excitements of passion and revenge.

It is an error, almost of universal recurrence, to consider human legislators as endowed with primary and original authority. Dazzled with the ostentatious parade of civil power, we mistake the feeble coruscations of the glow-worm, for the permanently powerful emanations of the sun.

The legislative authority of government is strictly declaratory, and not original or arbitrary. The laws of morality are antecedent to society, and constitute the universal basis of legislation. " Thou shalt not kill—thou shalt not injure thy neighbour," are the positive injunctions of that justice, which is co-existent with the universe. The earthly legislator may superinduce an additional sanction, but he cannot change the inherent character of the action. If the statutes of society are repugnant to the pre-established principles of the divinity, no terrestrial sovereign can render them of moral or political validity.

Nature of legislative authority.

There is however a circumscribed sphere, within which it is usually allowed, the lawgiver may exercise original legislation. Over that class of actions, which moralists have denomi-

Chap. VI. nated indifferent, it has been maintained, that he is entitled to exercise discretionary jurisdiction. The arguments in support of this doctrine, are possessed of captivating plausibility. Let them be submitted to the touchstone of examination.

The principal criterion by which we decide upon the nature of action, is the effect of which it is productive. Every particular action is a link in the universal chain of causes and effects, which must inevitably lead to the production of its consequent. Whatever is beneficial, should be assiduously cultivated. Whatever is injurious, should be carefully avoided. Justice regards the order and relations of society—she is willing to adapt her decisions to the condition of the social state. Invariably attentive to the relative situation of men, it is her province to enquire, what conduct under given circumstances, will prove most extensively beneficial? To pursue that conduct is precisely the substance of the law to be decreed. The discretionary power of the legislator consists not in an exemption from the jurisdiction of justice ; it is not a matter of indifference, whether the procedure most beneficial, is or is not prescribed. Duty is omnipresent. In the most express and forcible language, it will dictate to the legislator, " It is not within your discretion to determine, whether the path of benefit shall or shall not

Of human action.

Genuine province of the legislator.

be pursued. Your discretion is entirely confined CHAP. VI. to the discovery of what is in reality beneficial. That, and that alone, you are bound to decree."

Imagine it to be proposed as a law to prohi- An example. bit the exportation of corn. This is one of those subjects, over which it has been supposed the legislator is entitled to exercise original juris- diction. Let us examine the principles upon which such statute might be founded. If its considerations are in reality indifferent, the law would be immoral, inasmuch as it would be tyrannical to shackle society with unnecessary restrictions : but if those considerations furnish a ground for preference, then the legislator is bound to decide in favor of the benefit.

Let us enter into an analysis of the particular considerations in which such statute might be supposed to originate. Have our harvests been unproductive ? Is there a prospect of failure in our succeeding crops ? Is famine to be appre- hended ? In either of such cases, who will as- sert, that the decision to be made is unconnect- ed with the nature of morality ? Are our neigh- bours famishing with hunger ? Shall we refuse to afford them a supply ? Is there no morality in the intercourse of nations ? But let it be sup- posed, that we are in hostility with the state to whose ports such exportation is prohibited— how will that circumstance vary the nature of

CHAP.
VI.
the question ? Are we justified in the wanton infliction of injury, or in the omission of good offices, without receiving proportionable benefit ? It will doubtless be answered, that in this view the law is to be considered as one of the allowable methods of coercion. It will not be used as a blind and barbarous instrument of vengeance—its principal object will be to compel our enemies to desist from injury, and to render us the reparation to which we are entitled. But let it be enquired, from whence does such reasoning originate ? Is it not evidently derived from the school of ethics ? Is not the legislator bound to pursue the path which terminates in benefit ? How then shall it be affirmed, that he is independant of the empire of morality ?

Duty of
the legis-
lator.
It is perpetually the duty of the legislator to promote the welfare of society. If our conduct tends to the public injury, he is compelled in justice to exercise his prohibiting power. Neglect would be tantamount to a violation of morality ; but if our conduct is not injurious, it is immoral to interpose the shackles of restriction. Every unnecessary law is in its nature tyrannical—it is a wanton infringement of the rights of personal liberty and judgment. It renders political institution unnecessarily complex. It operates as a trap to the incautious—it will elude public attention and obedience, inasmuch as it is founded in principles wholly factitious

and arbitrary. There is no situation in which Chap.
VI. the lawgiver can be placed, in which he will not be furnished with substantial ground of preference. In whatever step he treads, the laws of justice and morality will closely pursue him.

From the internal administration of government, let us direct our attention to its transactions with respect to foreign states. In this department of our enquiry, war and negotiation are the principal subjects which are represented to our consideration. It is impossible that any war can exist in which one at least of the contending parties is not criminal. National hostilities present a horrid spectacle of the most aggravated calamity and guilt. We are too liable to become fascinated by the splendor with which military prowess and exploits have been too successfully decorated. Ambition and false glory, are the most fatal and pernicious of all the human vices. No palliative can be offered for wanton and unprovoked aggression—the offending party is perpetually guilty of the most flagrant violation of morality.

It is defensive war alone that can be justified before the stern tribunal of justice. The injury may already exist, or it may only be threatened. In either of these cases, it is equally the duty of government to avert the impending evil. When force is either menaced, or actually em-

_{CHAP.}
_{VI.} ployed, it is the province of the public guardian
to array and marshal the physical strength of society, to prevent or repel the aggression.   Upon what ground then shall it possibly be contested, that war is a proper subject of moral
disquisition ?

Nego-
tiation.   Negotiation is that intercourse or agreement
which takes place between governments for the
adjustment of differences, or for the regulation
of reciprocal concerns.   As for the secret intrigues between princes and cabinets, they are
nothing but a wicked conspiracy against the
tranquility and happiness of mankind.   It can
never be the true interest of one state to injure
another.   If governments were universally imbued with a love of justice, wars would never
exist, and there would seldom be any occasion
for negotiation.

Treaties.   Treaties are doubtless proper for the accommodation of differences existing between na-
tions.   In this case, they are applied to a temporary or to an extraordinary purpose ; but considered as a permanent standard for the regulation of conduct, their utility is in general exceedingly questionable.   They often tend to
embarrass and perplex the measures of a government, and frequently give offence to other powers.   Justice is a perspicuous and universal
principle, and abundantly sufficient to determine

the path which ought to be pursued. The
Statesman who is incumbered by numerous conventional stipulations, will find, that his task is
extremely complicated and difficult ; instead of
being guided by the evident rules of natural law,
and shaping his conduct according to the situation of affairs, and to the exigency of events,
he will often be reduced to the alternative of sa-
crificing the interest of his country to unreasonable compacts, or hazarding a rupture between
the parties.

It is scarcely possible, that any concern should
exist between nations, of which justice is not
the competent standard of determination. The
rights of every state, and its duties towards other
powers, are established in principles which cannot be controverted. The conduct of one state
towards another, can never be a matter of indifference ; nor can it be difficult to discern the
path most proper to be pursued, without the
intervention of any artificial regulations.

The stipulations comprised in a treaty, may
be considered in the following points of view :
first, as declaratory of the pre-existing principles of justice ; secondly, as contradictory or
repugnant to those principles ; and thirdly, as
altogether positive, and founded in considerations of reciprocal convenience.

1. In the first of these cases it is plain, that such convention does not produce the smallest alteration in the conduct which ought to be pursued by the respective parties. It confers no partial or exclusive privileges, and introduces no favoritism or invidious distinction. If then it only afforded additional certitude and energy to justice, it would be meritorious, and not reprehensible.

But we should ever consider the extreme impropriety, to attempt by previous declarations, to regulate that conduct, which should, in a great measure, be governed by future events. An instrument which only contains abstract principles, or propositions, must always be right, provided those principles or propositions are founded in equity. But what is in reality practical justice, must invariably be gathered from the circumstances of the case to which it is applied. Treaties, are never exclusively confined to the abstract enunciation of principles ; they also undertake to apply those principles to facts which are uncertain, because they are yet to happen. They contain an improvident engagement to act in a given manner, without considering in how eminent a degree the merit of conduct will be varied, by the difference of situation and incidents.

2. Conventions that are repugnant to justice are evidently indefensible. National intercourse should in general be governed by the same principles which regulate the intercourse of private life. Impartiality is equally a virtue in either case. The duties of humanity are of common obligation between every state. Sound policy will invariably dictate, that whatever rule of action is adopted, should be universally pursued. An engagement to consider one nation as the most favored, will render us obnoxious to the rest of mankind. Other powers will view us with a spirit of jealousy, which will ever be liable to ripen into discord, and to kindle into enmity. Our councils will be continually suspected of secret intrigues, duplicity, and partiality. They will be perpetually exposed to foreign machinations and seduction. Under the influence of such a system, the task of government will always be arduous and perplexed : it will be constantly distracted by the dissentions between foreign states, and incessantly attracted towards the vortex of hostility, by the unnecessary extension and complication of its political engagements.

3. It is almost impossible to consider any of the regulations contained in a treaty, as being entirely of an arbitrary nature, and independent of the jurisdiction of morality. It may indeed

be contended, that nations have the right to institute whatever rules may be agreed upon for
the government of intercourse, which do not violate or contradict the principles of justice : but
it will presently be perceived, that the hypothesis which maintains the indifference of any great
proportion of conduct, is liable to very serious
objection.   It is impossible that any general rule
can be adopted for the regulation of conduct,
which is entirely devoid of moral quality.   It is
impossible that any question of national concern
should be stated, in which the decision to be
pronounced is altogether indifferent to justice.
There is not an article which can possibly be
comprised within a treaty, which will not tend
to benefit or injury : in either case, its character must be ascertained by the standard of morality.   It is far from being denied, that nations
have the right of establishing such conventional
engagements as may be productive of mutual
benefit : but the true policy of partial engagements is in most cases questionable.   It is generally the wisest plan to treat every nation with
equal impartiality.   Exclusive privileges, and
partial regulations, have a tendency to divide
mankind into parties and circles ; and to produce artificial attachments, enmities, and interests, which are attended with the most injurious consequences.

If the conduct prescribed by a treaty is in reality beneficial to the contracting parties, why should not the same rule of action be extended towards the rest of mankind ? One of the principal objections to treaties in general is, the spirit of partiality and favoritism which they introduce. Considered in this light, they are perpetually hostile to that universal justice which should ever regulate the conduct of states. They introduce a system of confederation, and generate political relations, which give rise to what may be termed an unnatural state of nations.

There are few lessons more forcibly impressed by history, than that which teaches the inefficiency of treaties. Unless the finger of Interest points to rectitude, it will be vain to place any considerable reliance upon the written letter of conventions. No cabinet will forego an evident advantage, upon account of any positive stipulations, if it can only calculate upon strength sufficient to accomplish its designs. Wherever we can rely upon the justice of a foreign state, treaties are unnecessary : but if we cannot rely upon its justice it is plain, that we must either depend upon its weakness, or seek security from an unity of interest. The charge of punic faith, belonged to the Romans as well as to the Carthaginians ; and with equal truth it may be applied to the nations of modern Europe.

It is a question of very doubtful determination, whether treaties do not possess a greater tendency to occasion than to prevent hostility. They frequently excite the jealousy and provoke the resentment of States which are not parties. It is equally evident, that they furnish grounds of accusation between the contracting powers, which would not otherwise have existed. A voluminous series of engagements will always be liable to contradictory interpretation; and the injury complained of, instead of being impartially examined, and discussed upon the solid principles of justice, will be measured by the length and breadth of syllables. Language is imperfect; separate understandings may conceive the same term with material shades of distinction; the contracting parties are generally accustomed to converse in different languages; it is impossible to compose a system of multifarious engagements, with such perspicuity and exactness, as will preclude the parties from disputing with respect to its import and extent : treaties, therefore, instead of being a continual preservative of peace, are frequently fertile with causes of complaint and pretexts to quarrel.

It is by no means intended to assert, that treaties are in all cases improper; on the contrary, notwithstanding the preceding objections, they are sometimes highly expedient. As it is the common practice of nations to regulate their Chap.
VI. concerns by conventional engagements, it is sometimes necessary to comply with a practice so universally adopted. In a state of general society, more perfect and improved, no other rules would be required for the government of national intercourse, than such as are founded in principles of rectitude, which are obvious to every understanding. Even at present, the introduction of treaties may be considered as a hazardous expedient. The cautious and enlightened Statesman will use them as sparingly as possible. He will never be prodigal in promises and engagements. He will invariably rely much more upon the energy of justice, and the ligament of interest, than upon the feeble tie of words and protestations. He will generally abstain from committing himself, and becoming pledged to pursue a predetermined system of conduct ; but wisely remain at liberty to adapt his measures to events.

The ordinary objects of negociation may with Treaties. tolerable accuracy be comprised within the following division :—The restoration of peace— conventions of amity or alliance—and regulations of commerce.

Treaties which are exclusively intended to Of peace. restore tranquility, are of all others the most entitled to approbation. " War is an unnatural state of nations." It is a continued series of crimes and sufferings ; it is attended with incessant violation of the rights and duties of humanity. Peace is the restoration of intercourse and happiness. It is therefore the duty of government to fasten upon every opportunity to terminate the progress of desolation and slaughter. It is evident, that war can only be defended upon the absolute consideration of necessity. The moment that our enemy has ceased from his injustice, or the impending danger is removed, justice will decree that the ruthless hand of the destroyer shall be stayed.

Of alliance. Treaties of alliance are sometimes strictly defensive, and sometimes they contain engagements to unite in offensive operation. Treaties Offensive. of offence are immoral, for precisely the same reason that every unprovoked aggression is founded in injustice. The character of defensive. Defensive alliance will depend upon the objects it is intended to promote. Be it imagined, that weaker communities are placed in the neighbourhood of a powerful and ambitious prince ; that they are perpetually menaced with invasion, and exposed to encroachments : in such case, a convention to unite their forces for the purpose of repelling the meditated injury, will be meritorious ; it may present a front sufficiently formidable to ensure protection, and maintain tranquility, by deterring the hostile sovereign from pursuing a difficult and hopeless en- ^{CHAP.} terprise. But let it be supposed, that either of those contracting states, calculating upon a coalition of strength, should violate the rights of another power, and render hostility the only means of redress, would a case thus circumstanced be comprised within the terms of a treaty of defence? Who cannot perceive, that under this statement the merits of such compact, to say the least, would become exceedingly questionable? It is plain, that these considerations also are to be tested by the general standard of ethics.

Commercial treaties are generally used to regulate the rate of duties that shall be imposed upon merchandize. To designate what ports shall be open to the enterprises of the merchant —to stipulate what immunities shall be enjoyed by the citizens or subjects of the contracting powers—to define the articles which shall be comprehended within the rule of contraband— to furnish an opportunity for the safe removal of individuals and property, in the event of a future rupture. Such is the ordinary nature of the regulations they contain. Can it be denied, that such regulations are to be canvassed by the standard of moral investigation? In the first place, it is to be observed, that the merit of such conventions are to be estimated by the benefit they afford. As far as they are possessed

CHAP.
VI.
of a restrictive operation, either by the imposition of duties, an extension of the rule of contraband, or by any other provisions, the merit
of those restrictions is properly estimable by the
salutary consequences with which they are attended.   So far as they create additional privileges, the propriety of their stipulations is also
to be discussed upon the principles of natural
law ; or, in other words, by the application of
the same moral standard.

It is further to be remarked, that commercial
intercourse and relations are rather individual
than national.   Nevertheless, injuries affecting
the rights of commerce, although they immediately operate upon persons in their private capacity, are properly made a general cause.   Whether those infractions are the irregular and unau-
thorized acts of an individual, or committed under the auspices of a government, they are
equally irremediable by the interposition of municipal tribunals ; forasmuch as the inhabitants
of one community are independent to the coercion of the government of another ; and because
no common umpire is or can be established, to
relieve one citizen or state from the encroach-
ment of another.

These and similar considerations give rise to
the intercourse between governments, and introduce consuls, ambassadors, and envoys, as

the organs or agents of reciprocal communica- Chap. VI.
tion. Such ambassadors may be considered as
the advocates of their government or communities. It is their province to state, admonish,
and represent. When they complain of a certain injury, or state a particular grievance, they
reason and expostulate. The foundation of
their arguments must be established in the regula of equity, the stipulation of treaties, or the
laws of nations. Now what are the laws of nations, but a branch of the extensive science of
morality?

The law of nations is partly founded upon Law of nations.
the universal law of nature, and partly originates
in convention or agreement. With respect to
the former branch, it is clearly but another
name for that part of general morality which
respects the intercourse of states. The latter,
which is usually denominated the positive or artificial law of nations, derives its authority from
the efficiency of consent. Wherever its origin
cannot be distinctly traced, its evidences are to
be found in established usage, or in the text of
approved and judicious writers. In either of
those cases, it is equally maintained, that those
positive institutions are founded upon the basis
of stipulation, although the evidences of such
agreement have unfortunately perished. In this
light, we should consider that interesting code

CHAP.
VI. of positive law, which governs the political
transactions of the European world.

Moral code.
The first, or superior branch, which may pre-eminently be entitled the moral law of nations, is possessed of universal authority, because it is established in those universal principles of justice, which no potentate can change. The positive law of nations, being entirely founded upon convention, can only bind those particular states, who are the actual or presumptive parties to such convention. Such, it may be alledged, has been the case with all the sovereigns of Europe : because their uniform practice has been in recognition of that positive law. But whether distant empires, such as China, or the United States of America, are bound by its decisions, may at some future period become the subject of interesting speculation. Have the measures of our government already amounted to an acceptance of that positive law ? Or will considerations of policy enforce future acquiescence in its authority ?

Positive code.

Government subject to the moral law.
The validity of the positive code of nations, will also be dependent upon the empire of morality.   Whenever its positions are repugnant to the principles of natural justice, they are absolutely void. " If it contains any thing unjust or illegal, it is of no force ; and every nation is under an obligation to abandon it. Nothing being

able to oblige, or permit a nation to violate a natural law,"* it may be supported, as an uni-versal proposition, that the merit of such conventional code must ever maintain a perfect correspondence with the utility of its operation.

It appears, therefore, abundantly evident, that upon whatever theatre government is destined to be the actor ; whether in the ordinary routine of municipal affairs, or in the extraordinary intercourse with the constituted authorities of foreign states, the laws by which its conduct is governable, proceed from the same immutable source.   Universal justice, whose light is darted into every mind, must be the guide of its decisions, and the parent of its actions.   It is within the compass of the ordinary measure of understanding, to compare and estimate its proceedings, by the application of such unvarying measure of rectitude.

But here it will be interrogated, " How is it An objection from possible, that justice should decide upon the the indifference of merit of those positive institutions, which are certain adopted for the regulation of conduct, in mat-actions. ters that are indifferent ?   How can morality be applied to the examination of conventions which derive their obligation from the force of contract ?   How can it relate to those eccentric stipulations between particular states which have

* Vattel.

been established from motives of convenience, and not from principles of equity ?" It is by no means difficult to remove the objection arising from those considerations.

The preceding objection, is evidently derived from the postulate which maintains the indifference of a certain proportion of conduct. In the first place, it is extremely questionable, whether any of our actions can with correctness be denominated indifferent. Superficial observers have been too successful in the inculcation of an opinion, that among the infinite variety of our actions, there are many which hold a middle station ; and are so nicely balanced between the opposite extremes of virtue and vice, that they are, properly speaking, indifferent. This plausible conceit has been uniformly supported by writers whose inattention has prevented them from acquiring profundity in the contemplation of ethics. Most undoubtedly there are infinite gradations in the character of human actions. But, as every action is necessarily connected with its consequent, in the destined relation of cause and effect ; in the continual progress of events, it will most probably tend to some moral determination. Notwithstanding the link which unites the antecedent with its subsequent, may by its subtlety elude the vigilance of observation, it may nevertheless possess a real and powerful existence. Admitting that

the infinitesimal point of contact, which constitutes the relation between one action and another, is invisible or evanescent, is it not highly
presumptuous to conclude, that it has therefore
no reality? The character of actions is determinable by their immediate or intermediate, their
present or remote, direct or collateral consequences. It is perhaps impossible that those
inevitable consequences, should, during the
continued course of their progression, remain
entirely indifferent. Is it not most probable,
that they must in a greater or less degree, operate to the benefit or injury of some Being?
May not the opinion, that certain actions are
indifferent, be owing to our want of discernment with respect to their tendency? Is it not
certain, that when our discriminating powers
are rendered more subtile and acute, that many of our actions, which are now considered as
indifferent, will be discovered to possess a striking and distinguished character? But whatever question may exist, with respect to the indifference of particular actions, it is sufficiently
clear, that no general system of regula for the
government of conduct, is destitute of moral
character.

But secondly, admitting that a certain limited class of actions may be considered as indifferent; still there is no room to contend, that
national intercourse and regulations are com-

prehended in that class.   No affair of importance, no object of magnitude, can possibly be
viewed as indifferent.   It may be deemed of no
consequence with what my table is covered ;
but the rights of commerce, and the public concerns of state, must ever be entitled to the most
serious solicitude.

Thirdly, were it even maintainable, that commercial and national intercourse are properly
subjects of indifference, it would be far from
following, that the establishment of positive
rules for the regulation of those concerns, is
equally indifferent.   It is a sound position, that
the restraint of indifferent affairs, is tyrannical.
If it is said to be of no consequence upon what
aliment I subsist, it would then be an intolera-
ble oppression to interpose coercion with respect to my diet.

Fourthly, if it should be contended, that national conventions are to be vindicated upon the
ground of expediency ; viewed in that light,
consider what character they assume.   If they
tend to violate any natural right, they are undoubtedly immoral : if they tend to no beneficial consequences, they are also in a certain degree immoral ; because every unnecessary interposition of power, and every useless infringement of liberty, is contrary to justice.   Public
usefulness is therefore the exclusive standard of

decision ; and shall it be denied, that general utility is properly the subject of moral and political investigation ?

With respect to politics, justice is an universal standard, adapted to reach every conceivable case. Can, then, an exemption from its authority be claimed in favor of national conventions ? Shall it be maintained, that those stipulations possess the power of converting wrong into rectitude, or injury into equity ? We have seen that it may be questioned, whether any action can correctly be denominated indifferent, because every associated consequent, however distant or remote, enters into its moral constitution, and stamps it with a real and incontrovertible character. It is much more certain, that every instrument contrived for the regulation of conduct, whatever may be the subject upon which it operates, is the proper object of moral disquisition.

Univer-
sal autho-
rity of jus-
tice.

Suppose we instance the celebrated and much contested question, Whether it is expedient that the neutrality of a ship shall constitute a protection against the capture of its cargo ? Can it be said, that the determination of this question is altogether indifferent to morality ? Is it not the perfection of political ethics to direct its enquiries to the promotion of general happiness ? Does not a considerable proportion of the pros-

Examples.

CHAP.
VI.
perity of mankind, depend upon a just decision of the very question which is instanced? Examine the various treaties which have been established ; we find some to embrace the affirmative, and others the negative of this proposition. Is it possible, that stipulations so diametrically opposite, can be equally compatible with justice? Can we hesitate to decide, that one must possess an incontrovertible claim to preference, and that such preference is due to the decision most extensively beneficial? Shall we entertain even a momentary doubt, whether the compacts affixing a rule of contraband, are foreign to enquiries of morality? Are they not likewise the genuine subjects of similar disquisition? Wherever the mental eye can penetrate, or the piercing ray of understanding become directed, it will be found that the empire of morals has extended its benevolent and eternal jurisdiction.

From the preceding observations it must be
Applica-
tion.
evident, that the character of political institution depends upon the application of simple and perspicuous principles. The nature of internal legislation, and the merit of every system of jurisprudence, can only be ascertained by its concordance with justice, or its useful tendency. Indeed it may be maintained as a general proposition, that utility is the genuine and perpetual test of justice.* The true merit of laws,

* Godwin's Political Justice.

must always depend upon the benefits they pro- duce ; for whatever is extensively useful should invariably be enforced.

The transactions of states, with respect to each other, are governed by the principles of natural justice, or by agreements which take place between them. The first branch of this division comprises the moral and universal law of nations : the second not only comprehends the stipulations of treaty, but it likewise embraces the *positive* law of nations. The moral or natural law of nations, is founded in those principles of rectitude which are universal in their extent and obligation. The positive law of nations, and the stipulations contained in treaties, are founded in considerations of convenience. The *moral* law is supreme and paramount—the *positive* law is inferior and subordinate : the latter can never be valid when it is repugnant to the dictates of the former.

Man, as an Intelligent Being, is equally capable of discovering the laws that are founded in convenience, and those which are established in equity. As a Moral Being, it is his prerogative to investigate the merit of conduct, in whatever attitude, or upon whatever stage it is exhibited. The external transactions of states, and the internal superintendance of government,

CHAP.
VI.
equally furnish rules for the regulation of action. Whether the laws by which we are governed, are *moral* or *positive*, *general* or *particular*— whether they are considered to proceed from principles of justice, or considerations of usefulness, their operation and tendency is in every case to be discovered by that experience and reflection which are common to mankind.

CHAPTER VII.

THE SUBJECT CONTINUED.

Of Policy—Definitions of Policy—Whether man is capable of disinterested benevolence ?—Subtlety and infinite variety of motive—Harmony of the moral system—Justice and Policy compared—Applied to political affairs—Policy, as well as Justice, a familiar attribute—Application.

BUT here an objection presents itself, apparently of the most formidable nature. " Policy," it has been affirmed, " is the ruling principle of cabinets, which maintains a constant superiority over Justice, and governs with uncontroulable power the transactions of the public world. Policy is the polar star of princes ; it is the deity in whose temples and upon whose altars they constantly sacrifice every opposite principle." Such is the consideration which apparently augments the difficulty of state affairs, and furnishes an additional pretext for denying our general competency to investigate the transactions of government.

" The generality of mankind," say those objectors, " may indeed be competent to determine upon affairs of justice : still they are inadequate to pronounce upon the more complicated and eccentric questions of policy." " It is easier," continue they, " to decide upon the abstract justice than to determine upon the policy of any given proposition." Let us examine whether such objection possesses not more plausibility than substantial vigour.

What, then, is the distinction between Policy and Justice, and what are the points in which they resemble each other ? But let it first be premised, that the sacrifice of Justice to Policy is evidently criminal. The abandonment of universal good for partial convenience or private interest is most assuredly immoral. Such conduct cannot be the less flagitious because it is sanctioned or pursued by princes. Wherever the dictates of Policy are variant from those of Justice, the latter possess an incontrovertible claim to preference.

Defini-
tions of
Policy.   The term *policy* is frequently used as synonymous to cunning, subtlety, or art. In this li-

mited sense it has not the most distant connec- _{CHAP.} VII. tion with the merit of the object of pursuit: it barely signifies the possession of skill in the accomplishment of any design. When applied to the prince or the statesman, it is only an affirmation of his ingenuity or competency in the exercise of his profession. When we say that HENRY VII. of England, or CARDINAL RICHELIEU, were politic in their respective station or capacity, as king and minister, who cannot perceive that such proposition is entirely distinct from the possession of the moral virtues?

Policy, then, may mean the sagacious adaptation of means for the production of its end. In this sense, most certainly, its moral character is ambiguous: its merit in the school of ethics will altogether depend upon the laudableness of the motives by which it is actuated, or the intrinsic value of the object it is solicitous to obtain. It is, therefore, properly summonable before the tribunal of the moralist. That impartial forum will decide upon its character from the principles of equity.

Policy is founded in an attachment to Self: but Justice is the companion of Universal Benevolence. The former principally regards the prosperity of those by whom it is exercised; the latter extends its solicitude to the happiness of

mankind. The policy of a prince is directed to
the security of the prerogatives of his power :
the policy of a nation is exclusively devoted to
the promotion of its own particular and separate
happiness. In whatever degree policy may
have a tendency to benefit others, yet its considerations are not the less confined to self-in-
terest. If I render service to another from a
politic motive, such conduct is clearly distinguishable from that which originates in benevolence. The favor is evidently not intended to
him, but to myself. Justice, on the contrary,
is extensively beneficent : it would decree, perhaps, the very same benefit ; but from motives
more pure, exalted, and disinterested.

But Policy, in its more extensive and honorable signification, is not entirely confined to the
adaptation of means for the promotion of a particular end : it likewise implies a judicious
choice of the object we are desirous to obtain.
It signifies accuracy of discernment in appreciating the true value of that object, and estimating its effect upon our future happiness. In
this refined and liberal acceptation, it is synonymous to wisdom or prudence ; and differs from
Justice rather in the incentive by which it is actuated, than in the conduct it pursues. When
we act from considerations of policy, we study
our own good : but when we act from a love of
justice, our attention is extended to the good of

mankind. The moral system of the universe Chap. VII. has in reality wisely united general good with individual interest. However False Policy may prefer the gratification of a limited and momentary desire, at the expence of more valuable enjoyments that are permanent and future ; Sound Policy, whose comprehensive view explores futurity, and who constantly pursues the most solid and substantial blessings, will invariably perceive that true felicity is only to be found in the practice of virtue.

It has been pretty generally maintained by moral writers, " that man is not capable of disinterested benevolence ;" and that our most sublime and exalted conduct, when brought to the rigid touchstone of examination, will infallibly be traced to the passion of self-love. If we instance the memorable virtues of a CODRUS, LEONIDAS, FABRICIUS, or TIMOLEON, we shall be told that their love of glory and distinction were superior to the energy of patriotism and philanthropy ; and that the essence of pure and unalloyed virtue can never be extracted in the crucible of human nature. When those celebrated men either sacrificed themselves for the good of their country, or displayed a sovereign contempt of riches or of power, they are said to have been actuated more by the thirst of fame, than by a disinterested attachment to the cause of humanity or virtue.

Whether man is capable of disinterested benevolence

CHAP.
VII.

Subtlety
and infin-
ite variety
of motive.

There is no subject of disquisition more subtle than the nature and character of motive ; and the difficulty becomes increased by the consideration that our conduct originates from a complicated mixture and variety of incentive. There are few actions which are capable of being traced to the operation of any single motive. There are few sentiments which do not proceed from distinct though correspondent feelings. The pleasure we derive from the society of an amiable friend, will partly originate from the esteem which is commanded by his virtues, and partly from the personal gratification we derive from the charms of his conversation. Our exertions of magnanimity and fortitude may in all probability be traced to a variety of associated incentives : they will partly originate in an attachment to the cause in which they are exerted, and partly flow from the satisfaction we receive in becoming the candidates of honor and distinction. True virtue cannot require that men should become totally detached from themselves. The path of rectitude is covered with the choicest flowers of happiness ; the laws of the moral universe exhibit the most beautiful

Harmony
of the mo-
ral system.

harmony of design, and display the most universal benevolence of intention : they have decreed that felicity shall be the constant reward of virtue ; and that the same conduct which ensures our own substantial good, shall also contribute to the general benefit of mankind.

From these considerations it will appear, that Justice and Policy, however they may differ in the motives by which they are actuated, will pronounce the same decision whenever the same question is presented under identical circumstances. If it is objected that Policy is selfish, and that the nation which is implicitly governed by her dictates, exclusively studies to promote its own separate and particular interests. To this let it be answered, that it never can be Sound Policy in any government to inflict extensive injury on mankind. Every nation is equally interested in the preservation of those sacred elements of morality which cement the order and harmony of the universe. Oppression and Injustice, however they may dazzle the eyes of deluded tyrants ;—however they may contribute to the splendor of momentary power—can never be reconciled to the existence of substantial and durable felicity.   In their progress they are attended with an ever-active poison, which will corrode the fountain of authority, and pollute the manners of the people. The infection will infallibly fasten upon the vitals of society, and only terminate its ravages with the final dissolution of empire.

But what, alas ! shall we say of that complicated and enormous mass of injustice which has oppressed or desolated almost every region of

_{CHAP.}
_{VII.} the globe? We are actors upon a stage on which Vice has assumed a bold and dauntless front. How is it possible to avert the injuries by which we are perpetually menaced? Until the golden age of the poets is completely realized, and the delusive " day dreams" of Fiction are embodied into substantial existence, our conduct must be moulded and adapted to correspond with the present features of political society.

Admitting that a government is disposed to regard the rights of neighbouring states with the most implicit veneration, can it reasonably promise itself that its neighbours will be constantly governed by the same spirit of justice and moderation? Must it not be perpetually guarded and fortified against the aggression and hostility of foreign nations? Is it not a duty of the most imperious necessity, that it should be vigilantly prepared to oppose its powers of resistance to withstand the injuries and desolation with which it is continually threatened?

Applied to political affairs.   Is it Policy or Justice to which we must resort for the solution of such questions? We have already perceived that it is an inseparable characteristic of Justice to shape and accommodate its decisions to the existing situation of affairs; and that it will perpetually direct us to pursue our own interest and happiness, whenever such

pursuit does not militate to the injury of others. CHAP.
Neither Justice nor Sound Policy will ever compel us to acts of wanton and unprovoked aggression : but they will equally command us to exert our talents with constancy and fortitude for the preservation of every valuable right.

But it will be alledged that nations frequently submit to regulations, intrinsically unjust, from motives of accommodation, or from conciliatory principles. It is not unusual for governments to bend to error, or yield obeisance to imposition or prejudice. But why do they thus submit ? From no other consideration than because the evil is too powerful for their imbecile means of resistance. Such considerations resolve themselves into questions of political arithmetic. The proposition becomes stated, Whether it is better to submit to certain unjustifiable pretensions of a foreign power, or by resistance incur the more extensive calamities consequent on war ? Now let it be imagined that application is made to Justice or to Policy to prescribe the conduct most proper to be pursued : what are the grounds upon which the decision will become suspended ? Most undoubtedly the aggravated nature of the injury. The relative military force of the parties, the evils which are incident to submission on the one hand and to hostility on the other, will be nicely weighed and balanced in the scale of deliberation. It is evident that such proposition implies a prudential choice between evils ; and that, whether Justice or Policy is the arbiter to decide, their judgment will strictly correspond in directing us to pursue that conduct which will produce the lesser evil, and ensure the greater benefit.

Such, then, is the accurate distinction between Policy and Justice. It remains to be examined whether the medium of human capacity is not as capable of discussing the dictates of the former, as it is competent to the discernment of the laws and axioms of the latter.

Policy a general attribute.   It has plainly been perceived that Justice and Policy equally regard the consequences of Conduct ; that the former considers Conduct as it relates to the general happiness of mankind, and the latter as it concerns our individual interest or that of the particular community whose welfare engages our solicitude. It has also been established, that Judgment is a property of mind possessed in common by every Intellectual Being. It is unquestionably the province of Judgment to consider the consequences of Conduct in all its relations. Experience is the parent of Knowledge. Shall it be said that it teaches us the effect of action upon the general happiness of mankind, but leaves us blindly ignorant of its operation upon our personal con-

cerns? Is it not palpably evident that the discovery of what relates to our own interests must
have preceded the discernment of what concerns the interest of others?

Policy is a general and familiar attribute. Application.
Craft and Prudence are in a certain degree common to all men : they all possess the faculty of
calculation ; they are habitually prone to penetrate into consequences ; Experience enables
them to explore into the recesses of futurity ;
they possess the habitude of prophecy as well
as the gift of speech. The pursuit of Interest is
the universal incentive of mankind ; and the
means of effecting that design are the substance
of our earliest lessons in the extensive school of
society. How, then, shall it be contended,
that Man, whose pre-eminent characteristic is
Intelligence, and whose moral constitution is
Thought—whose life is a continual series of
action, and whose time is measured by the succession of perceptions—shall be doomed to constant ignorance of those laws and that conduct
by the discipline and operation of which his
happiness is perpetually affected ? Upon what
plausible ground shall the position be maintained, that he whose existence is unceasingly connected with a continued train of action and experience—whose mind is habitually exercised in
discovering the consequences of his actions—
whose proceedings necessarily originate from

CHAP.
VII.
deliberations of the understanding, matured and ripened into volition—shall be eternally ignorant of those laws of Justice or of Policy by which his conduct is invariably governed?

Government is principally conversant in the regulation of the usual routine of affairs, and the subject of that morality which is perceptible to every understanding. It follows, as a necessary consequence, that the character of its measures is legible to the generality of observers. Where, then, are the depths and diversified windings of Civil Policy too dark and inscrutable to be fathomed by common minds, too sacred to be submitted to the unhallowed inspection of the vulgar? Are they comprised in the question already touched upon, Whether it is more expedient to pronounce a declaration of war, than to remain in the secure tranquility of peace? What are the usual considerations which enter into the decision of such question of expediency? What is it but a plain and perspicuous enquiry of calculation, which in its solution only requires a pertinent and comprehensive statement of the case? If our national rights have been infringed by foreign hostility, what citizen remains ignorant of the extent of the provocation? The injury is the occasion of repeated conversation and reiterated complaint. Shall it be said that the public are ignorant of an injury to which they are themselves the victim?

Will it be affirmed that any man is ignorant of
that which from its nature is an object of universal notoriety ? Shall war, then, be resorted
to for the obtainment of redress ? What individual is deprived of the scale which balances the
evils of hostility on the one side, and the benefits proposed on the other ? Every man is sufficiently acquainted with the value of the prize at
stake. Considerations of national right, and
even of national dignity, are familiar to the
mouth of a peasant. Every person is competent to appreciate the concomitant miseries of
war : Experience has associated them in every
understanding. It is known that blood must
flow, and treasures become expended ; it is
understood that the public debt will become
enlarged. As for taxation, it is a matter of primary sensation. The soldier who follows expe-
riences the general misfortune in as great a degree as the officer who commands. Perhaps,
indeed, every understanding will not become
alike familiarized to the whole complicated ca-
talogue of evil : it may not have duly considered the moral consequences of war ; it may not
have estimated its operative effect upon the machine of civil government. Hence it is that a
certain degree of implicit confidence will ever be
reposed in administration. Nevertheless the
individual must be something inferior to an Intellectual Being, who is unable to form a tolerably correct idea upon the subject.

CHAP.
VII.

The question of preference between Peace
and Hostility is of extraordinary occurrence.
In proportion as it involves more extensive and
important considerations, its decision is the more
complicated and difficult. It cannot be denied
that the various grounds of preference upon
which such decision depends, are present to
every mind, and in some degree familiar to every understanding. No room, therefore, can exist for contest, that the medium of human capacity is sufficient to pronounce upon topics of
inferior magnitude : such are most measures of
interior jurisdiction, which involve consequences of much less hazard, and with regard to
which mistakes are readily susceptible of remedy.

It has been the artifice of Despotism to enve-
lope its measures with the sable mantle of mystery, and to awe the wondering multitude with
the unsubstantial phantom of delusive subtlety
and refinement. Like the Eleusinian rites, or
the oracle at Dodona, its emoluments and its
existence have depended upon successful imposture and pernicious delusion. However
complicated and extensive may have been the
doctrines relating to Government, an accurate
and philosophical analysis of the subject will reduce the nature of its superintendance to plain
and perspicuous principles. Notwithstanding
the artificial refinements with which the hand of

Ostentation or the dangerous designs of Impos- Chap. VII.
ture may endeavour to complicate or disguise
them, those principles will ever remain open to
the ordinary comprehensions of mankind. It is
the duty of Science to review the art of Legislation, to correct its imperfections, and remove
its deformities. It is the province of Wisdom
to erect the political edifice agreeably to the
rules of solid and rational Architecture.

CHAPTER VIII.

On the perfect Right of Individuals to communicate their
Sentiments upon Political Topics.

Corollary from the preceding doctrine—Source
of political power—Government dependent upon
the general will—Of public opinion—Necessity
of freedom in its formation.

THUS far it has been attempted to
establish the perfect right and ability of society
to enter into the discussion of political topics.
It will be perceived that the subject has hitherto been considered upon general grounds, and
entirely independent of any particular system of
social institution. We will next proceed to examine how far the reciprocal intercourse and
communication of opinion upon those topics is
a right attached to individuals ; and whether
any, and what, restrictions should be imposed

CHAP.
VIII. upon the exercise and enjoyment of such right.
We shall afterwards, in some measure, retrace
the subject of the present treatise ; and consider
it, in the first place, with relation to representative governments in general—and, secondly,
as it particularly respects the Constitution of the
United States.

Corollary   The right of individuals to discuss political
from the
preceding questions, is a corollary necessarily derived from
doctrines. the doctrines which have been established in
the preceding chapters : for as individuals are
the elements which enter into the composition
of society, the general rights of a community
must be considered as a common bank or ag-
gregate, of which each of its members is entitled to his *peculium*. When we assert that Society is possessed of the absolute right to investigate every subject which relates to its interests,
it would be palpably contradictory to deny that
every individual possesses the same right in the
most perfect and extensive acceptation. The
position which maintains the general right of a
commonwealth to exercise the freedom of political discussion, intends that such is a common
privilege appurtenant to each of its members.

Source of   Government itself must evidently have been
political
power. derived from the pre-existing *rights* of Society.
It is, accurately speaking, an organ of the general will, intending to answer particular and ap-

propriate purposes. It is clearly the right of _{Chap.} _{VIII.}
Society to institute such regulations as may best
promote its own particular interests, prevent
the perpetration of offences, and designate the
laws by which its members shall be governed.
The exercise of this right is indispensably requisite to the preservation of its existence : but as
Society is incapable of exercising that right in
its collective or corporate capacity, it was necessary to designate and select the particular
persons who should represent and exercise its
powers for those purposes. It has already been
sufficiently established, that general delegation
is the only legitimate basis of Government. Social Institution is the organ which represents the
rights of a community in a limited degree. It
is only possessed of those rights which are either
expressly conferred, or those which are necessarily presumed to have been delegated : those
which are retained by Society are open to the
exercise of each of its individual members.

It has already been perceived that however _{Govern-}
extensive may be the powers of government, _{ment de-} _{pendent}
its existence must essentially depend upon the _{upon the} _{general}
determination of the general will.* Whatever _{will.}
may be the particular form which it has assum-
ed, it is equally the organ of Society, instituted
for the promotion of the public welfare. In
every case it is responsible to the people for the

* Chap. II.

faithful performance of the trust committed to
its charge. It is perpetually liable to dissolution by the same power from which its origin is
derived. Society, therefore, in its original capacity, possesses a revisionary right : as such
right is altogether independent of positive institution, and incapable of delegation, it must
ever remain the subject of individual exercise.

The general will, which is the necessary result
of Public Opinion, being superior to Political Institution, must of consequence remain independent of its controul. Governments are entrusted with the exercise of the ordinary powers of
sovereignty : but Society is, nevertheless, the
real and substantial sovereign.

It becomes an enquiry of the most extensive
Of public
opinion. importance, to discover the precise meaning to
be affixed to the extremely complicated term
Public Opinion. Does it imply the opinion of
Society in its collective and organized capacity ?
Or does it designate the union or aggregation
of individual sentiment ? How are we to determine what is in reality the general opinion of a
community ? Where shall we seek for its evidences ? Where shall we listen to the voice that
can express it ?

Society does not constitute an intellectual unity ; it cannot resolve itself into one single or-

ganized percipient, in which the rays of Intelligence are concentrated and personified : each
of its members necessarily retains his personal
identity and his individual understanding. By
Public Opinion we are, therefore, to imply an
aggregation of individual sentiment.

It is the individual who is to reflect and
decide. By Public Opinion we are to understand that general determination of private understandings which is most extensively predominant. When a sufficient number of the
members of a community have established a coincidence of sentiment upon any particular subject, such agreement of their personal judg-
ments may be correctly termed the general or
Public Opinion. When they have concurred in
volition upon any given point, that concurrent
volition may be denominated the public or general will. Unless such prevalent opinion or
volition of individuals constitutes the public opinion or will, the conclusion would be inevitable that it is impossible public will or opinion
could exist.

The evidence of public opinion may be either positive or presumptive. In the former
case it may be gathered from the express declarations of the people : in the latter it is to be implied from their silent acquiescence. It is true
that " the million" cannot possibly assemble

CHAP.
VIII.
for the purpose of deliberation : but still their
opinion upon momentous occasions may be taken at the separate assemblage of districts.
Suppose a proposition to establish the authority
of an absolute monarch should be submitted to
the American republic, for the purpose of deciding upon this subject ; all the active members of the community might be summoned to
attend the meeting of their respective towns.
At such meetings every individual might deli-
ver his sentiments and pronounce his will. It
is probable, that upon most subjects some dis-
senting voices would be found. Perfect unani-
mity is seldom to be expected. But in a true
practical sense the opinion of the majority is to
be deemed the general opinion.

It is equally true that the current of public
opinion must always be presumed to pursue a
direction in favor of established institutions.
The general acquiescence which is paid to the
laws, and the uniform submission and obedience
observed towards the government, must be received as conclusive testimony that they are supported by public opinion.

We are not, however, to imagine that any
thing which deserves the name of Public Opinion exists with respect to every subject of re-
search. There are some topics upon which an
uniformity in sentiment is pretty generally esta-

blished : there are others which may be considered as being in the infancy of discussion. The
formation of general opinion upon correct and
salutary principles, requires the unbiassed exercise of individual intellect ;   neither prejudice,
authority, or terror, should be suffered to impede the liberty of discussion ; no undue influence should tyrannize over mind ; every man
should be left to the independent exercise of
his reflection ; all should be permitted to communicate their ideas with the energy and ingenuousness of truth.   In such a state of intellectual freedom and activity, the progress of mind
would infallibly become accelerated ; we would
all derive improvement from the knowledge and
experience of our neighbour ; and the wisdom
of society would be rendered a general capital,
in which all must participate.   Exposed to the
incessant attack of Argument, the existence of
Error would be fleeting and transitory ; while
Truth would be seated upon a basis of adamant,
and receive a perpetual accession to the number of her votaries.

But here it may be affirmed, " that diversity
of sentiment is the constant lot of imbecile and
erring mortals :" how, then, shall such consideration become reconciled with the existence
of what is denominated Public Opinion ? If
contrariety of judgment is perpetually the con-

dition of society, to what party shall we attribute
the intellectual, and with it the political ascendency ?   It is in the first place to be observed,
that the tendency of such objection will be rather to abridge the extent than to annihilate the
existence of Public Opinion.   The idea conveyed by such compounded expression, is peculiarly abstruse and complicated ; it combines the
perception of all the infinite variety of knowledge, together with the separate decisions of a
multitude of independent understandings.   If
there are many subjects of disquisition in which
the determinations of human intelligences are
dissonant and diversified, numberless are the
truths which have established an undisputed
and universal empire.   In proportion as investigation continues free and unrestricted, the
mass of error will be subject to continual dimi-
nution, and the determinations of distinct understandings will gradually harmonize.   Upon
every subject that can become presented to our
attention, it is the province of Reason to deliberate and determine.   The uninterrupted progression of Truth demands that the intellectual
intercourse between men, should remain entirely unshackled.   No ideas of terror or restraint should be associated into the discussion ;
no foreign consideration should enfeeble or perplex the judgment ; mind should be compared
with mind, and principle weighed with principle.   Introduce the incessant habit of indepen-

dent reflection, and the establishment of Public
Opinion upon a rational and salutary basis will
follow as the necessary consequence.

It is likewise to be remarked, that diversity
of sentiment in the earlier stages of enquiry, is
far from being unfavorable to the eventual reception of Truth. It produces Collision, engenders Argument, and affords exercise and
energy to the intellectual powers ; it corrects
our errors, removes our prejudices, and strength-
ens our perceptions ; it compels us to seek for
the evidences of our knowledge, and habituates
us to a frequent revisal of our sentiments. In
the conflict between opinions we are enured to
correctness of reflection, and become taught in
the school of Experience to reason and expatiate. It cannot surely be visionary to predict the
ultimate triumph of Truth. Whatever may be
the oscillation of principles, the pendulum is finally destined to rest at the salutary point of
Rectitude. Many are the considerations which
may accelerate, and numberless the causes that
may retard the melioration of society. In the
midst of every obstacle that presents itself to be
encountered by Fortitude, it is a source of ne-
ver-failing consolation, that Mind has already
proceeded too far to retrograde. Prejudice may
boast of her fascination, and Tyranny may ex-
ult in his chains ; Superstition may administer
the slumbering opiate, and Delusion continue

CHAP.
VIII. to practice her magical artifices : the rays of Intellectual Light will still proceed to brighten and increase, and the days of Liberty and Science succeed to the gloomy night of Ignorance and Despotism.

CHAPTER IX.

The same subject considered from the revisionary powers of society.

Nature of revisionary power—How to be exercised—Of a secondary delegation—Idea inadmissible—Of individual exertion—An objection—Answered.

Two important propositions may be considered as established: the first, That Government is the instrument of Society, intended to promote the general purposes of its ordination; the second, That Society must always possess the perfect right of determining how far such instrument has answered the designs of its institution. From those considerations it is clearly to be inferred that Society should incessantly maintain a species of censorial jurisdiction over its political institutions. Let us proceed to examine in what manner a community must exercise such *revisionary powers*.

How to
be exer-
cised.   Shall it be said that a nation in its collective capacity is competent to the exercise of deliberation? Most assuredly not. Such position would destroy the necessity, and therefore undermine the whole theory of delegation: for why should we appoint organs for the transaction of affairs to which their constituents are sufficiently competent?

There are only two alternatives submitted to our choice: individuals must either be permitted to investigate and decide upon political measures; or Society must constitute an additional organ, invested with the right of controuling its political institutions, and empowered to exercise the province of a censor over government.

Of a secondary
delegation.   Shall, then, the revisionary right of Society be exercised through the medium of secondary delegation? Shall an assembly be appointed to pronounce upon the merit of the transactions of government, with authority to weigh the validity of its laws in the scale of morality—to estimate the propriety, ascertain the justice, and consider the policy of its measures? Shall an organised tribunal be erected to compare and examine the statutes of the legislature with the

paramount standard of a constitution? Most
undoubtedly not.   It would be impossible to
imagine a more flagitious and terrible expedi- The idea
ent.   No device could be more dangerous, or inadmissible.
pregnant with such complicated calamity.   It
would be the establishment of an *imperium in
imperio* : it would unite in one tremendous engine all the dreadful powers of Despotism and
all the direful evils of Anarchy.   What guardian genius could shield us from the tyrannical
operation of so unexampled an assembly? Is it
possible that Public Liberty should receive additional security by such enormous multiplication of power? If government is necessary, shall
its momentum be arrested by the impetus of a
disciplined body perpetually moving in an opposite and hostile direction?   Would such assembly imbibe the spirit of Patriotism, or acquire
the incessant habitude of Disorganization?
Should the operation of laws become suspended
until such unheard-of tribunal had pronounced
upon their validity?   In cases of determination
diametrically different, whose decision should
become adopted? Should such assembly possess
the power of putting a *veto* upon the measures
of the government? So absurd an expedient
would perpetually maintain the banners of civil
war, and establish a permanent sanctuary of
faction and rebellion.

CHAP.
IX.

Individu-
al exer-
tion.

It is evident, then, that no other salutary method can be adopted, to enable Society to investigate the measures and correct the abuses of Government, than to enlighten and increase the perceptions of individual Mind. Knowledge is capable of being communicated : every mean should, therefore, be embraced to render its illumination of extensive utility. There is no species of tyranny more pernicious in its consequences than that which is exerted to impede the progress of Intellect. Society has no other resource for the melioration of its condition, and the improvement of its political institutions, except what is derived from the reciprocal communication of Thought, and the increasing energy and correctness of individual Understanding.

All our prospects of improvement must therefore depend upon the industry and exertion of individuals. It is almost impossible to conceive the extensive effects which may be produced by the agency of a single person. One enlightened and active mind may create a light which by a series of fortunate incidents may irradiate the globe. Instead of palsying the efforts of individuals, it should rather be our study to enlarge their powers. Instead of checking the ardour of Enquiry, we should endeavour to stimulate and encourage the activity of Mind. In an exanimate or depressed state of society, there is

but little chance of meeting with exalted intel- CHAP.
IX.
lectual powers ; and, even if they should exist,
they would seldom be furnished with the opportunity of rendering extensive benefit to the community.

Slavery will inevitably produce mental debi-
lity and degradation.   Unless the mind is conscious of liberty to reflect and expatiate, it will
be wholly incapable of sublime and energetic
exertion : but if it can freely exercise its facul-
culties and impart its thoughts, it will be warm-
ed and animated ; inspired by the sublimity of
its emotions, it will perpetually increase in vigour and information.

Wherever Freedom of Enquiry is established,
Improvement is inevitable : the smallest spark
of Knowledge will be cherished and kindled into flame.   If only a single individual shall have
acquired superior attainments, he will speedily
impart them to his companions, and exalt their
minds to the elevated standard of his own.
There is something peculiarly captivating in the
acquisition of knowledge.   The communication of learning affords perhaps equal pleasure
to the preceptor and the scholar.   Emulation
is natural to man : it will always prompt to study.   Competition will ever lead to unremitted
industry ; Science will increase the number of

CHAP.
IX.
her votaries ; and rising students will continually improve upon the knowledge of those by
whom they are preceded.

It would be vain to expect that Government
should in any eminent degree contribute to political improvement.   It is only to be wished
that with respect to the improvement of general
Science it would observe strict neutrality. There
is no other method to multiply and disseminate
knowledge than by the exercise of reason. Government does not possess any extraordinary or
peculiar powers of logic : its distinguishing property is Force.   It is better qualified to exercise the office of an Executioner, than to assume
the province of an Instructor.

The true utility of Government is to suppress
crimes and afford protection to the community:
every other interference is pernicious, and will
be continually liable to abuses.   The magnet
will lose its properties sooner than magistrates
will cease to aim at an extension of prerogative.
Unless a principle of melioration exists in Society, Political Institution will assuredly degene-
rate.   If Government is destined to become improved, the power by which it is amended must
act independently of its controul.

An objection against the Freedom of Political Chap. IX. Enquiry, has been derived from the ignorance of certain societies. Men who are immersed in ignorance and barbarism are said to be unqualified for the enjoyment of Liberty. As they are but little exalted above the brutes, they are incapable of comprehending Reason, and must therefore be governed by Force. A nation of barbarians will be prone to vice and disorder ; it will be turbulent, restless and discontented : it must, therefore, be awed into submission by the Herculean energy of Government. Military establishments, rigid penalties, dungeons, racks, and gibbets—in short, all the complicated terrors of Absolute Monarchy—are indispensible to maintain tranquility in a rude and uncultivated state of Society.

Objection, from the ignorance of certain Societies.

It is evident that this is to reason in a circle. If Ignorance furnishes an apology for Despotism ; Despotism, grateful for the favor it receives, perpetuates Ignorance. As it is the unvarying practice of Tyranny to interdict that investigation which is the only mean of knowledge and improvement, the nation now enslaved must never aspire to the blessings of Freedom and Humanity !

Answered

Let it be enquired at what happy æra did Despotism become an instrument of enlightening the public mind ? When was it the godlike

attribute of kings to destroy the pernicious dominion of Ignorance and Error? What monarch, since the age of HERCULES, has exerted his strength to combat Wickedness and Oppression? It is not the nature of princes to become imbued with patriotic sentiments: their
constant solicitude is directed to the splendour
of Authority, the gratification of Ambition, and
the enjoyment of Factitious Pleasures. They
feel that their personal interests are hostile to
the public good; they are conscious that the
imperfections of society compose the strong
foundation of a throne; and, in proportion as
they are attached to Prerogative, they breathe
inveterate hostility to Talents, Truth, and
Virtue.

It is unquestionably necessary that Government should possess sufficient energy for the
suppression and coercion of Vice; it is further
admitted, that a ferocious and unpolished people should be controuled by powerful institutions: but, then, the energies of Government
should be properly directed; its authority should
be constantly interposed to prevent violence and
crimes, and never exerted to restrain that circulation of knowledge and sentiment which is essential to general improvement.

If it is contended that Ignorance produces
Vice, Ferocity, and Disorder, and that there-

fore the nation which is immersed in barbarism CHAP.
IX.
should be governed by the severity of Coercion;
let it be enquired to what object should such
coercion become directed ? Shall it be confined
to the suppression of crimes ? or shall it be extended to prevent the dissemination of that
knowledge which is the only salutary and efficacious corrective ? Severity, at the best, is but a
temporary expedient ; it is not calculated to effect a radical cure of the complaint.   Despotism
may be a proper instrument to punish, but it
will never enlighten or instruct : instead of rendering mankind more wise and virtuous, it will
have a perpetual tendency to subject them to
servitude and ignorance.

In an imperfect and uncivilized state of society, two principal objects will engage our solicitude—the prevention of violence and offences, and the improvement of the people.   The
first of these objects must be particularly submitted to Government ; but the other must be
entrusted to Society itself.

To promote the improvement of Society it is
essential that Mind should be free.   Unless individuals are permitted to reflect and communicate their sentiments upon every topic, it is impossible that they should progress in knowledge.
If we are not suffered to impart our information
to others, it is evident that such information

CHAP.
IX.
must remain useless and inactive. Without establishing the liberty of enquiry, and the right of disseminating our opinions, it must always be our portion to remain in a state of barbarism, wretchedness, and degradation.

It has sometimes been maintained, that in an unenlightened state of Society the toleration of enquiry is dangerous to the existence of Government : but the reverse of this proposition is in reality true. Ignorant nations are most prone to faction and intestine commotions. It is the want of Information which renders them liable to seduction. They feel the smart of Despotism, and blindly rush to the banners of Violence at the call of any intemperate and popular leader. Every established Government will necessarily possess the power of contributing to the public welfare. If we experience the evils arising from the imperfections of Society, Freedom of Enquiry will prompt us to submit with gratitude to the benevolent hand which administers the remedy : it will teach us to consider Government as our powerful protector. Investigation, so far from paralysing its efforts, will perceive the salutary tendency and absolute necessity of its operations. It will contribute to the security of its power ; and, by gradually enlightening the public mind, diminish the difficulty of its task.

The suppression of Vice must ever be necessary to the public welfare. It is impossible that Society should be the enemy of its own interest ; it is impossible that it should become hostile to the Government which is its constant benefactor.

However unenlightened may be the condition of a people, if they are accustomed to receive protection from the magistrate—if coercion is never interposed except to redress injuries—Government will unavoidably be rendered popular ; and the freedom of communicating our sentiments, so far from being dangerous to its existence, will be the best preservative of its powers.

It is not to be expected that nations will advance in improvement unless the interest of Government harmonizes with their own. If it is admitted to be a political maxim, *That the quantity of power must bear an exact proportion to popular ignorance,* as it is the interest or the constant disposition of Despotism to increase its prerogatives, it is evident that Despotism will exert its utmost vigilance to perpetuate the ignorance of its subjects.

Tyranny is the inveterate enemy of Truth. It is jealous of Talents ; and will ever continue to employ all its force against every principle

CHAP.
IX.
and every individual that might illuminate the understanding of its vassals.   This is not Declamation : it is serious and impressive Reality Shall it be said that the Emperor of the Russias is not opposed to the advancement of Literature ?   Can it be denied that his prerogatives have been exerted to prevent the progress of Learning and Civilization within his extensive dominions ? The chaste and elegant writings of Dr. Moore—the " Gustavus Vasa" of Brooke —the " Town and Country Magazine"—and the " Monthly Review," among many other volumes of real merit and unexceptionable morality, are not permitted to circulate in that land of darkness and slavery.*   The conduct of the

---

* Vide the " Monthly Magazine and American Review," published in New-York, and printed by Messrs. T. & J. Swords, for September, October, November, and December, 1799; which, among many other useful articles of Literary and Philosophical Intelligence, contains an account of some of the publications lately prohibited in the Russian empire.   It mentions that " all the censors at Riga are Russian Priests, who know no other language but their own ; for which reason every book which requires a licence to be imported must be previously translated to them.   If they suppose they have discovered something objectionable in a book, it is confiscated immediately, and committed to the flames.   One of the young Livonians, who returned this summer (1798) from Germany, took the splendid edition of Wieland's works with him. Unfortunately a volume was taken up for inspection, which contained something that appeared to the Priest to militate against the tenets of the Greek church ; and the volume, with its beautiful prints, was instantly thrown into the fire, which spoiled the whole set, worth twenty-six guineas.   Whole leaves are cut out of the foreign newspapers before they are circulated ; and it is even said that they are to be prohibited entirely ! ! !" Reader, make your own comments.   If your heart contains a chord which vibrates in unison with Humanity, cease to venerate a Tyrant.

Russian monarch, so far from being singular or
extraordinary corresponds with the uniform policy and practice of arbitrary governments.

The interest of Society requires that such Government should be established as is most favorable to the dissemination of Knowledge : for if
Information is prohibited, mankind must ever
expect to remain in a state of abject stupidity
and servitude ; Tyranny will ever retain its apology, and Tyranny will exist for ever. An ignorant people may indeed require a Government
of superior energy : but certainly the general
interest demands that such energy should be directed towards its proper object. In such case
Investigation can never be dangerous to its existence. The progress of Information will always be favorable to the salutary powers of Government : it will only be hostile to the crimes
and imposture of Tyrants.

The Revisionary Right of Society is not peculiar to any particular form of civil institution :
it is an inherent and fundamental right of our
social existence, which neither time, nor place,
nor circumstance, nor positive or arbitrary regulations can destroy. The pursuit of Truth and
Happiness is an eternal law of our moral and
intellectual nature, which Governments are
bound to reverence. Political dominion is esta-

CHAP. IX. blished for no other purpose than to suppress the commission of crimes, and to afford protection to the community. The coercion of Thought, and the restriction of Intellectual Intercourse, are entirely foreign to the sphere of rational jurisdiction. Society cannot delegate its revisionary powers to any special organized assembly : those powers can only be exercised through the medium of personal deliberation. If Ignorance and Stupidity are the condition of a people, no other remedy can be furnished than the exercise of Reflection and the unrestrained circulation of Opinion. The result of these considerations is inevitable : they must either submit to the eternal empire of Oppression, or establish the Freedom of Investigation in the most comprehensive extent.

CHAPTER X.

THE SUBJECT CONTINUED.

Communication of sentiment considered as a personal right and duty.

So far we have viewed the Intercourse of Sentiment upon political subjects as it principally relates to the general interests of Society. We are now to examine the question with more immediate relation to the personal rights and duties of Individuals.

1. Man as a moral and intelligent Being, is inseparably possessed of certain absolute and perfect rights. One of the most important and essential of those rights is the liberty of exercising his faculties agreeably to his own perceptions of what is proper and desirable, provided such exercise of his faculties does not tend to the injury of others.

Our Natural Liberty terminates at the precise point at which our conduct becomes injurious. Independent of the sanctions of Civil Institution, we never could claim the right of inflicting evil upon others. It is the principal end of Society to prevent and redress our wrongs, to protect us in the enjoyment of our natural rights, and not to abolish or destroy them.

Truth may be considered as the property of every Intellectual Being : it is the vital principle of Mind, and the only element in which our percipient powers can maintain a healthful existence. We have all a common interest in its illuminations ; we are all entitled to pursue it in every shape, and upon every subject in which it becomes presented.

The exercise of our mental faculties is as necessary to our existence and happiness as the employment of our corporeal powers. When we cease to reflect and speak, it may emphatically be affirmed that we cease to live.

2. Improvement is a constant law of our intellectual nature. Knowledge is a general fund, of which all have a right to participate : it is a capital which has the peculiar property of increasing its stores in proportion as they are used. We are entitled to pursue every justifiable method of increasing our perceptions and invigo-

rating our faculties.   We are equally entitled to communicate our information to others.

My neighbour possesses an inestimable volume, which is capable of unfolding some of the most serious and impressive truths : Shall I solicit his permission to peruse it ? He is a man of superior learning and penetration ;—the book contains a certain mixture of Falshood and Error ;—he has weighed and examined every principle it maintains ;—perhaps his understanding has enabled him to improve upon the author ;— he has enriched the subject with the fruits of original discovery ;—he presents me the book, with a friendly admonition to guard against its errors ;—he explains the principles it contains, and imparts the improvements which have originated from his personal meditation : shall I not listen with reverence to my intellectual benefactor ?

But, behold ! the volume is a Treatise upon Morality—upon General Politics !—In what shape does its consideration become varied from that circumstance ? There is not a subject more interesting to my mind, or more calculated to influence the tenor of my conduct : my future happiness, perhaps the tranquility of those upon whom my behaviour may operate, will essentially depend upon the rectitude of the opinions I imbibe.   But the volume also contains a va-

riety of observations upon the measures of Government ;—it investigates the particular character of PERICLES, and PERICLES is a principal agent of the administration : am I the less
entitled, upon such account, to examine its contents ? Is it not of importance to me that I
should be acquainted with the truth ? Can the
character of PERICLES be a matter of indifference, when it is PERICLES who is to direct
and govern those measures upon which the general prosperity depends ?

Shall I hesitate to pronounce my sentiments
upon such subjects ? Shall Terror prevent me
from affording them the most extensive publicity ? Are those sentiments true, or are they
founded upon erroneous information or deduc-
tion ? In either case, imagine that my intentions
are pure ;—I am actuated by no sinister incentive ;—Truth is the unrivalled object of my
pursuit : shall I be restricted in the method of
communicating my opinions ? Shall I be permitted to express in conversation what I am
prohibited from publishing through the medium
of the press ? If my impressions are true, their
circulation will be beneficial : if they are false,
it will be the means of destroying them. Should
my errors be confined within the private reposi-
tory of my breast, perhaps they may never be
removed : the poison may corrode my moral
constitution, and gangrene into guilt. The

publication of those errors will eventually produce a beneficial tendency ; it will infallibly be
the prelude to their detection.   But if my sentiments are founded in Truth, why should they
be concealed ?

An individual, who possesses the most exalted station in society, was the author of a work,
entitled, " A Defence of the American Consti-
tutions :" can it in any degree vary the merit of
those volumes that he has since their publication become President of the United States ?
Shall I be prevented from exploding their errors,
or discerning their mistakes, from considerations
of his official elevation ? At what period shall
the sentiments of a President become inviolable,
or his opinions be rendered absolutely infallible?
Shall such singular privilege be dated from the
accession to office ? or shall it possess a relation to any anterior period ? Suppose the sentiments contained in a President's writings are
identical with those which are comprised in his
addresses to the legislature : shall I be permitted to controvert the one, and yet debarred from
reasoning against the other ? Shall it be said
that an identical proposition can be right and
wrong at different periods of time ? Is Truth to
be obtruded by the rigorous despotism of Authority, or discovered by the faculties of the understanding ? If the empire of Intellect has no
connection with Civil Institution, why should

the idea of Magisterial Infallibility be associated with our moral and political disquisitions ?

3. We have also seen that our natural and
social existence presents a system of continual
duties. It is incumbent upon me, from a consideration of the various relations in which I am
placed, to exercise my faculties for the production of the greatest sum of good. I am bound
by the most positive precepts of Morality to cultivate my perceptions, and increase my powers
of discernment for the purpose of extending my
means of utility. There is not a situation, in
which we are capable of being placed, which
does not render us subject to particular obligations. It is not a matter of indifference whether my endeavours are directed to the cultivation of my mental faculties, or whether my time
is languished in sloth and supineness. It is not
indifferent to Morality whether I conceal the
perceptions of Truth within the dungeon of So-
litude, or whether I apply its evidences to remove the errors of my companion. We are not
entitled to waste our hours in lethargic inexer-
tion. True Virtue will stimulate us to a career
of unvarying vigour and activity : it will direct
us to pursue the incessant improvement of our
powers, and to employ them for such purposes
as are most extensively beneficial.

It is undoubtedly a duty of superior magnitude that we should assiduously endeavour to
cultivate our talents.   It is an obligation of
equal importance that we should strive to eradi-
cate our errors.   In proportion as our abilities
become extended, we are rendered capable of
useful exertion.   Our errors and prejudices not
only mar our usefulness :   they also render us
dangerous, and are perpetually liable to afford
a pernicious direction to our conduct.

4. There is no subject more interesting than
Politics ; there is none in which every individual is more extensively concerned, or which
may with greater correctness be considered as a
common property.   We are perpetually subject
to the influence of its institutions.   It is a matter of pre-eminent importance that we should
be acquainted with the nature of the regulations by which we are perpetually governed.   It
is a right of the most perfect and positive kind,
that we should possess and exercise the means
of discerning whatever contributes to our benefit or may destroy our happiness.

If the acquisition of Knowledge is meritorious,
it is virtuous to direct the strength of our understanding to the investigation of questions most
extensively connected with the prosperity of Society.   Politics is a subject of universal concern :

it relates to objects of public utility. We are equally interested in supporting the genuine principles of Social Security and Happiness. We are entitled to investigate every question which concerns the Public Prosperity. We are equally entitled to communicate the result of our enquiry and deliberation. He who conceals a treason against Society, is scarcely less culpable than the traitor who meditates its ruin.

Of all the rights which can be attributed to man, that of communicating his sentiments is the most sacred and inestimable. It is impossible that the imagination should conceive a more horrible and pernicious tyranny than that which would restrain the Intercourse of Thought. Who is not aware that much of the happiness of intelligent and social Beings consists in the pleasures of unrestrained conversation, the charms of security, and the sublime delight of communicating their ideas with a confidence unmingled with terror? Deprived of this invaluable privilege, Society loses all its charms, and abdicates its most exquisite enjoyments: it no longer possesses the genial power of unfolding the buds of Science, and awakening the choicest energies of Mind.

It was an observation truly worthy of the greatest of poets, that "The moment which makes Man a Slave takes half his worth away."

Liberty is the only vivifying principle that can Chap. X. animate his intellectual faculties, expand his mind, and invigorate his virtues.   The atmosphere of Tyranny is stagnant, gloomy, and condensed : it chills the embryo Thought, and blasts the young Perception.   By shackling the circulation of Sentiment, O Legislators ! ye close the avenues to Knowledge and Improvement, destroy the blessings and the virtues of Social Life, and reduce the human species to a condition but little more elevated than the ferocity and barbarism of brutal nature.

CHAPTER XI.

Of Restrictions upon the Intercourse of Opinion.

*Truth and Falsehood——Restrictions vindicated
from the pernicious tendency of Falsehood—
Restrictions opposed—Reasoning applied to a
virtuous Government—Falsehood to be combated by Truth—Licentiousness destructive of itself—Pernicious tendency of Coercion.*

CHAP.
XI.

I⊤ is an important object of our enquiry to discover whether the interests of Society require that any restraints should be imposed
upon the freedom of political discussion ; and to
ascertain whether any judicious method can be
adopted to guard against the evils of licentiousness on the one hand, and those of Despotism
on the other.

In the first place it is to be observed, that the Truth and
falsehood.
communication of Truth, so far from being cri-

CHAP.
XI. minal, should ever be viewed as eminently meritorious.   He who combats a pernicious error,
or destroys a dangerous Falsehood, may chal-
lenge a seat among the principal benefactors of
mankind.   The law which coerces the circulation of Truth cannot be vindicated upon any
principle of justice, or reconciled to any rational
theory of government.

Falsehood is constantly pernicious: wilful
Defamation is invariably criminal.   No man
can have a right to utter an untruth concerning
another: he is as little entitled to misrepresent
the public measures of a government.

In the present state of society it would be
fruitless to expect perfection.   We are often reduced to the necessity of choosing between opposite evils.   Whatever determination is most
nearly allied to the general good, should constantly be preferred.   It cannot be denied that
Licentiousness is injurious: but it is extremely
to be questioned whether the severity of criminal coercion is the most salutary and judicious
corrective.

The reasoning of the present work will be
exclusively confined to a consideration of the effects of Misrepresentation in public or political
transactions.   The Defamation of private character stands upon a separate and distinct foun-

dation. Personal transactions are not the sub- CHAP. XI.
ject of general concern or notoriety : the individual whose reputation is aspersed sustains a
personal injury. Attacks upon private character in general proceed from malignant or vindictive motives : they are calculated to affect
our private avocations and property. The prosecution which is commenced to redress the injury entirely assumes a civil complexion : the
object it embraces is Reparation rather than
Punishment.

What are the evils to be apprehended from Restrictions vindicated.
the aspersion of public characters, and from the
misrepresentation of political transactions ? It is
usually observed, with considerable vehemence,
" that the person of the civil magistrate should
be regarded with reverence, and his reputation
approached with deferential awe. How is it
possible to separate the person of the Public
Officer from that respect which is ever due to
Government ? The consequence of attacking
his reputation will be to render him odious and
suspected. Remove that esteem which is challenged by his personal virtues, and that confidence which should constantly reward his integrity, and you will infallibly lessen or destroy
his means of usefulness ; his authority, instead
of meeting with obedience, will become openly
controverted and contemned, or perhaps expose
him to insult and derision. The true founda-

tion of the power of Civil Government is the
respect and reverence with which it is generally
contemplated : to strike at that foundation is to
aim at the dissolution of Order and Peace in
Society."

Restric-
tions op-
posed.   Such is an epitome of the arguments generally advanced in support of the interposition of
Restriction, and such the alarming picture
which they usually represent.   Whatever spe-
ciousness may be attached to this reasoning, it
exhibits a perpetual libel against the character
and discernment of Society.   It argues a want
of confidence in the energies of Truth, and supposes that its evidences are less powerful and
captivating than the dominion of Prejudice and
Error.   He who contends that Misrepresentation will not invariably yield to the artless, simple, and unvarnished Tale of Truth, is egregi-
ously ignorant of the nature of Understanding,
and the genuine principles of the human heart.

The government which is actuated by corrupt
and ambitious views, it will be readily admitted, has every thing to apprehend from the progress of Investigation.   The authority of such
government is entirely founded in Imposture,
and supported by Public Ignorance and Credu-
lity.   It is, therefore, the interest of Tyranny,
as it values its existence, to deceive and hood-
wink the multitude.   The empire of Despotism

is founded upon Delusion, and is wholly irre- ^{Chap.}
concilable with the liberty of political discussion. XI.
Corruption considers Truth as her inveterate
enemy ; Talents and Virtues are regarded as
her most formidable antagonists : but shall it
be contended that the perpetuation of Imposture is to become the object of our anxious solicitude ? or that the interests of Society will
suffer by our ceasing to respect those fatal institutions to which Probity and Integrity are the
devoted victims—those pernicious systems upon whose altars the Liberties and Happiness of
the people are incessantly sacrificed ?

Public Good must constitute the exclusive
object to the attainment of which our enquiries
should ultimately be directed. To reverence
Oppression and Imposture is wholly incompatible with considerations of general prosperity.
The interests of Society require that the dominion of Despotism and Error should become
subverted. To sympathize with Tyranny is a
refinement in cruelty : it is to abandon every
exalted feeling of our nature, and every noble
attribute of humanity. If it is the province of
Investigation to enlighten the public mind, and
destroy the abuses of Political Institution, it
should be assiduously cherished, and esteemed
as the most powerful benefactor of mankind.

CHAP.
XI.   In examining the true merits of this subject,
we should therefore confine our attention to a
Reasoning Government which is uniformly actuated by the
applied to
a virtuous love of justice, and impressed with a constant
Govern-
ment. solicitude to promote the general happiness.
Wherever such a Government exists, it is plain
that every proceeding which can embarrass its
operations, and diminish the respect to which
it is justly entitled, will lessen its authority and
usefulness, and materially injure the interests of
Society. It remains to be enquired whether a
Government of that description can entertain
any serious apprehensions of the effects of misrepresentation; and whether a more judicious
remedy than the coercion of a criminal code
cannot with confidence become applied?

It is an incontrovertible position that a Government which is steadily actuated by an ear-
nest and sincere desire of promoting the public
good must infallibly possess the confidence of
the people. It has been already maintained to
be impossible that Society should ever become
its own enemy.* The will of a community
must always be directed to the general benefit.
If Truth is sufficiently powerful to combat Falsehood and Error, it should become a principal task
of the honest and enlightened statesman to present its evidences to public view.

* Chap. 9.

Is it to be imagined that where an admini- ^{CHAP.} stration is possessed of the qualifications which must necessarily secure its popularity, any misrepresentation of its measures should obtain an extensive reception, or become attended with mischievous consequences? Such supposition would inevitably imply either a want of integrity or remissness in duty. The idea of a Government uniformly actuated by laudable and patriotic sentiments, is diametrically opposed to Mystery and Concealment. Publicity is one of the principal characteristics of its proceedings; Truth, Sincerity, and Justice are the pillars upon which it is supported. A stranger to Artifice and Dissimulation, it feels no apprehension from popular emotions; it shrinks not from the eye of general observation; it acknowledges Responsibility to be an active, efficient, and substantial principle, and continually presents to public view a perspicuous and circumstantial history of its conduct. Fortified and emboldened by the consciousness of upright intention, it considers itself invulnerable and secure. Confidence is mutually reciprocated between the Government and the People. In proportion as the public mind becomes habituated to discussion, it is rendered more enlightened and informed. In proportion as political measures are accompanied with the evidences of rectitude, and enforced by the energy of reasoning, the general mind becomes invigorated and correct-

ed ; and misrepresentation has little prospect of
obtaining an extensive circulation or reception.
There can be no room for jealousy and suspicion
where nothing is mysterious and concealed.
Faction is confounded and appalled by the powerful lustre which surrounds a system of Virtue.
In vain shall Malevolence direct its shafts at the
venerable guardians of Liberty and Justice :
thóse shafts will become enfeebled and shivered
by the contact, or recoil with a redoubled momentum upon the hand by which they were
propelled. Wherever Sincerity is an acknowledged attribute of the Government, and the
civil magistrate becomes accustomed to exhibit
an undisguised and faithful account of his measures ; wherever a community is accustomed to
the uncontrouled exercise of political discussion,
its confidence in the wisdom and integrity of its
public officers will become strengthened and
increased ; and it will be impossible to stimulate the people to intemperate opposition, or to
render them the dupes and the victims of designing conspirators.

It is true that every individual possesses an
appropriate sphere of influence and activity ;
and that his sentiments, and even his errors,
will possess a certain quantity of weight upon
those with whom he is ordinarily conversant.
But will it be maintained that the prejudices of
a few individuals are sufficiently powerful to in-

fect the general mass of opinion ? Shall it be ad- _{CHAP.}
mitted that the erroneous sentiments of a limited
circle can ever be dangerous to a Government
erected upon the solid adamant of Political
Truth? Whatever might be the malevolent
views of a few ambitious and interested conspirators, it is impossible that any respectable proportion of the community should become cor-
rupted with hostile and treasonable designs.
Nations can never become benefited by decep-
tion.   It is their eternal interest to pursue the
direction of Truth and Virtue : their errors,
therefore, must continually appertain to the understanding, and not belong to the heart.

What, then, are the most judicious means of
preserving the Government from the wanton attacks of Licentiousness; and what the best security of Public Liberty against the hostile encroachments of Ambition? It will be found,
upon an accurate examination, that the same
remedy is equally adapted to the removal of
each of those evils.

Such remedy is to be found in the extensive _{Falsehood}
dissemination of Truth.   But what is the most _{to be com-batted by}
efficacious method of obtaining the universal re- _{Truth.}
ception of Truth ? It has hitherto been the prac-
tice of short-sighted Policy to combat Falsehood
with Force.   Coercion may, indeed, be adequate to the purposes of punishment : but it

never can be rendered the instructor of mankind.   If you entertain the beneficent intention of removing my errors, and correcting my
mistakes ; if you wish to banish my vices and
purify my heart, assume the salutary office of
the preceptor ; speak to me with kindness and
clemency ; tell me in what I am wrong, and
point to the path of rectitude.   Under such circumstances, can it be possible that I should refuse to listen with complacency ? If you are
sufficiently impressed with the importance of
your subject, the generous glow of enthusiasm
will animate your mind ; and you will infallibly
become imbued with captivating eloquence.
There is a chord in every breast attuned to rectitude.   Reason and Argument, whenever they
are properly applied, possess the power of pe-
netrating into every understanding : but nothing can be more injudicious or more at war
with its own purposes than the application of
Force.   Instead of attracting, it perpetually re-
pels ; it engenders Animosity and Opposition,
and naturally inspires distrust.   The penalties
of positive Law may awe me into silence ; they
may perpetually bear down the energies of
Mind : but they are better adapted to become
an engine of Oppression, than a happy instrument for the promotion of Political Virtue.

Considered as the means of counteracting the
injurious effects of Falsehood, the interposition

of a penal code is altogether unnecessary. On Chap. XI.
the other hand, it is invariably attended with the
most pernicious and dangerous consequences to
Society : for most assuredly it is of equal importance that we should guard against the encroachments and abuses of Government, as that
we should endeavour to prevent the evils of licentious Misrepresentation. Criminal law is
invariably liable to be exerted as an engine of
Power : it may be used as the instrument of an
administration for the purpose of crushing those
individuals whose sentiments are viewed as obnoxious. Can we always be secure in the independence and impartiality of the tribunal by
whom it is administered ? Will judges never
lean in favor of those constituted authorities
which are the fountains of patronage and preferment ? Will they never be inclined to sacrifice a victim upon the altars of Power? Will
they carefully abstain from vindictive incentives,
and from the infliction of aggravated and exor-
bitant penalties ? In fine, are not more complicated and tremendous calamities to be apprehended from the introduction of coercive restriction than from the most unbounded licentiousness ?

How, then, shall erroneous opinions or wilful misrepresentations be combated by the wise
and provident legislator ? The proper answer to
this enquiry is, That Government should by no

means interfere, unless by affording such information to the public as may enable them to
form a correct estimate of things. Let us suppose an idea is circulated, that a certain measure of administration is likely to produce calamitous effects, or that it has originated from flagitious and dishonorable designs. It will be
contended that such an idea will be injurious in
proportion to the extent of its circulation. Admitted. But how shall such opinion be destroyed, or its farther propagation prevented ? By
fair and argumentative refutation, or by the terrible dissuasive of a statute of sedition ? By the
convincing and circumstantial narrative of Truth,
or by the terrors of Imprisonment and the singular logic of the Pillory ?

Licenti-
ousness
destroys
itself.   It is the constant tendency of Licentiousness
to defeat its own purposes. In a state of Society, which admits of continual and unrestrained
discussion, the triumph of Falsehood can never
be of permanent duration. There is no character which excites general obloquy and detesta-
tion more readily than that of the malignant Slanderer. In proportion as the public mind becomes inured to the exercise of Investigation, its
discriminating powers will be rendered discerning and correct ; it will become enabled instantly to distinguish between Truth and Error ; every man will be taught to reverence and fear the
enlightened judgment of the community ; De-

tection will closely pursue the footsteps of Mis- Chap.
XI.
representation ; and none will dare to fabricate
or utter the tale of Falsehood with impunity.

The nature as well as the policy of Civil Government requires that confidence should be reposed in the wisdom and virtues of the people.
Prudence, as well as Magnanimity, will dictate
that it should uniformly rely upon the established sanctity of its character. An extreme perti-
nacity in analysing syllables, and a jealous sensibility at the approach of Censure, naturally
creates the suspicion that there is something vulnerable in its constitution, " *something rotten in*   Pernici-
the state of Denmark." If it is in reality traduc-   dency of
ed, it will invariably possess the means of vin-   Coercion.
dicating its honor without resorting to the ambiguous infliction of punishment. Any erroneous sentiment that may prevail with regard to
its administration can readily be removed by the
salutary application of Argument. Error in the
public sentiment respecting the affairs of Government arises in every instance from the want
of information in the community : it is, therefore, in a great measure, attributable to the
mistaken polity of administration itself, in con-
cealing the necessary means of knowledge. Let
a Government accustom itself to the publication
of a succinct and accurate detail of its measures,
with their operation and inducements ; no room

will then remain for misrepresentation ; dema-
gogues, who calumniate from criminal incentives, will become instantly silenced and confounded ; and the honest but misguided victims
of their artifice will relinquish their prejudices
upon the first approach of the superior evidence
of Truth.

Besides, as far as we suppose that men are
actuated by views of personal interest, Government will never want its champions and vindi-
cators : a croud of panegyrists, like the army of
POMPEY, will be readily collected by a stamp
of the foot : for " wheresoever the carcase is,
there will the eagles be gathered together." Patronage and Office, that " hope of reward"
which " sweetens labour," will always multiply
the advocates of authority. Government will
ever possess an imperious advantage in the argument, without resorting to the auxiliary power of criminal jurisprudence. There are more
that will always be ready to vindicate than to
censure its measures from selfish or sinister considerations.

The restrictions which are enforced by the
authority of a penal code will always possess an
ambiguous character. In their nature they are
liable to perpetual abuse : they can only be necessary to support a Government whose measures cannot survive the contact of Investiga-

tion.   It is sufficiently apparent that the Government whose established reputation of virtue
has secured the veneration of the people, is invulnerable to the shafts of Calumny : it cannot,
consequently, be driven to the expedient of obtaining security through the severity of its criminal system.   Restrictions upon the Freedom
of Investigation must, therefore, be repugnant
to every rational theory of Political Institution,
and pregnant with the most unsalutary consequences.

We would deceive ourselves by imagining
that a system of Restriction is possessed of a
negative character ; that if it cannot produce
much benefit, at least it will not be attended
with any considerable evils.   On the contrary,
it ever will be accompanied by the most positive and formidable mischiefs.

It will be the continual tendency of such system to damp the ardour of Political Enquiry,
and. to inspire the mind with terror.   The investigation of public measures will incessantly
be associated with the dread of prosecutions and
penalties ; and the apprehensions of fines and
imprisonment will every where pursue us.   In
vain shall we attempt to estimate the precise
extent of prohibition, or ascertain what we are
permitted to speak, and at what point we are
compelled to silence : the expressions of an un-

CHAP.
XI.
guarded moment, the innocent communication of what we have learned from another, the confidence we repose in the information of a friend, may be tortured into guilt, and subject us to the evils of oppressive and unmerited punishment. The censorial jurisdiction of Society, which can only be rendered useful so long as it continues independent and unrestricted, instead of being a powerful guardian and preventative against abuses, will only serve to amuse the people with the semblance and unsubstantial shadow of liberty; while in reality it will constantly expose the zealous and upright advocate of popular justice to the vindictive and acrimonious persecution of authority.

The system of Restriction is an awkward expedient of securing the confidence of the People, or promoting the popularity of the Government. A statute of sedition may stifle the open declarations of dissatisfaction, but it will ever be liable to strike the disorder into the internal and vital parts of the social frame. It is but illy calculated for the permanent establishment of tranquility, or for effecting a radical cure of the complaint. In a community accustomed to the enjoyment of any considerable proportion of Freedom, that which cannot be ingenuously spoken will be secretly and bitterly murmured. Government will constantly participate in the terrors it has inspired. The moment the first sensations of surprize become extinguished, Discontent will acquire the redoubled energy of an ANTÆUS, and exert the many hands of a BRIAREUS. The latent fire may cease to flame, but it will not cease to exist. Feeding upon suppressed and hidden, yet powerful combustibles, it will again burst forth, extend, and consume, with all the irresistible and convulsive fury of a volcano.

CHAPTER XII.

THE SUBJECT CONTINUED.

Unity of design essential in political systems—
Restrictions considered in the shape of punish-
ment—-Improper and unnecessary—-Inter-
course of Opinion, the only preservative of Li-
berty—Public Opinion—Should be independent
—Danger of investing Government with means
to controul it—Objection from the necessary
secrecy of particular transactions—Answered
—Further remarks.

A POSITION of the most serious
magnitude is, that Political Institution should
exhibit unity and harmony of design. It is impossible to engraft the regulations of Slavery
upon the trunk of Liberty, without altering the
nature and properties of the tree. One system
or the other must inevitably acquire the ascendency. If the frequent prosecution of libels

should excite discontent, Government will finally become compelled either to relax from its
severity ; or, what is more to be apprehended,
will be driven to fortify its powers by the introduction of a Military Despotism.

We have already seen that the Restriction of
Political Opinion, by the powerful arm of Government, is susceptible of the most dangerous
abuses, and incessantly liable to be prostituted
to the most invidious and oppressive purposes.
Shall we, then, to prevent an inferior and almost imaginary evil (an evil which is constantly
pursued by a salutary and efficacious remedy)
resort to the introduction of a system which may
be accompanied with such formidable calamities ? While we extend our solicitude to the
suppression of Licentiousness, shall we cease to
remember that the Freedom of Investigation is
pre-eminently requisite to guard against the
abuses of Authority ? In the exuberance of our
zeal against malignant Calumny and Misrepresentation, shall we consent to paralize and crip-
ple the most beneficial powers of Society ?
While we are contemplating the vices and the
frailties of mankind, shall we totally forget that
Governments are abundant partakers of the passions, temptations, and infirmities of our nature ?

It is generally imagined that political expediency requires the libeller to be punished.
" Shall the slanderer of Government be suffered
to triumph with impunity ? Shall he not meet
with the severity due to his misdeeds ?" There
are a variety of considerations which may be offered as conclusive answers to such interroga-
tions.

We must carefully distinguish between the
defamation which relates to Private Individuals
and that which concerns Government. In the
first case a personal injury is sustained.—Private
Character being tender, and not an object of
notoriety, is susceptible of suffering from Misrepresentation. The erroneous impressions of a
single man may be extremely pernicious to another. The prosecutions commenced for Personal Slander are founded in real damage: they
aim at redress; they are entirely the objects of
civil jurisdiction, and are not liable to become
converted into instruments of oppression.

Our attention must therefore be confined to
the Defamation of Government. Misrepresentation of the character or transactions of administration is viewed as a public offence: it is,
therefore, contended that it should be punishable, as well as every other crime of a public
nature.

CHAP.
XII.

Improper.

In reply to such doctrine, it is to be observed, that the advancement of public good is the true principle upon which all crimes ought to be punished. Coercion should not be exercised for any other reason than because the conduct which is to be restrained is injurious to the community. He who perpetrates a robbery, or is guilty of fraud, commits a real injury, which will not admit of apology. The punishment of such offences is always necessary, and is never subject to abuse : but the interference of Government, to punish men for their assertions respecting itself, ever has been, and ever will be, subject to the most odious oppression.

Public prosecutions for libels are, therefore, more dangerous to Society than the misrepresentation which they are intended to punish. We should be cautious of entrusting Government with a weapon which may render it invulnerable. It has already been contended, that Punishment, abstractedly considered, is a multiplication of human calamity.* It should never, therefore, be resorted to, unless from momentous considerations of general utility. Few doctrines are more pernicious than that which contemplates the infliction of injury as the only effectual reformer, and pains and mutilation of the body as the best expedient to purify the

* Chapter 2.

mind. The inhuman error has originated in
palaces, and has insinuated itself into families
and schools.   If the same ingenuity and fervour
had been employed to enlighten the intellectual faculties, as has been exerted for the refinement of cruelty and vengeance, the world
would have been advanced much nearer to maturity ; and Virtue, instead of Terror, would
govern our conduct.

It has been rendered sufficiently plain, that a Unneces-
virtuous Government cannot become materially sary.
injured by Misrepresentation : for the most acrimonious and violent invectives will be the
most open to detection. Why, then, should
punishment be inflicted ? Will the confinement
of my body within a prison, or the removal of
my property to the public treasury, render me
a better man ? Will such severity be calculated
to conciliate my affections towards the Government ? or will it be likely to inspire me with
lasting resentment ? If I have been guilty of
malicious detraction, let corroding Envy, sick-
ening Jealousy, and vulture Passions torture
and prey upon my heart. Believe me, I should
be punished by misery more aggravated than
the horrors of an inquisition. He who attacks
Truth will be sure of disappointment : he will
be shunned, detested, and, like CAIN, will be
sentenced to wear a mark of infamy upon his
brow. If I have mistaken the character of an

CHAP.
XII.
influential personage, or misconceived a particular transaction of Government, my mistake
should be corrected by Reason, and not by the
laceration of my body. If I have wilfully mistated the measures of administration, or uttered
malevolent invectives against a public officer,
Coercion cannot be necessary to vindicate the
character of the one, or to remove an erroneous
impression with regard to the other. If punishment is intended for the gratification of personal
revenge, it is evidently immoral : if founded in
considerations of general utility, it is the offspring of mistaken theory. To remove an erroneous impression, nothing more is necessary
than the unequivocal representation of Truth.

Government should only inflict punishment
with reference to public views. As our actions
respect ourselves, we should be left to our con-
sciences and our GOD. No position can be
more true, than the popular maxim, that " it is
better ninety-nine guilty individuals should go
unpunished, than one innocent victim be sacrificed upon the shrine of criminal law." There
is no subject so delicate as the declaration of
our opinions. Nothing can be more difficult
than to pronounce with certainty upon the sincerity of the man who may have mistated the
transactions of Government. How can it be ascertained what portion of actual Malevolence
and how much of mistaken Zeal, existed with-

in his mind ? Shall I be imprisoned for creduli- Chap. XII.
ty, or fined upon account of my imbecility of
understanding ? Shall we punish mankind for
their prejudices and mistakes ? Shall the enthusiasm of honest Opinion be scourged and fet-
tered, because it squares not with the political
standard of the cabinet ? In the midst of my
errors upon topics of general concern, it is more
probable that I am actuated by upright design,
than governed by the settled incentive of premeditated guilt. How, then, shall we discriminate between undesigned Mistake and wilful Misrepresentation ? Shall a Court of Starchamber be erected in the bosom of Society, to
decide upon the import of particular phraseology, and determine what given proportion of
acrimony pervaded the bosom of the speaker ?
In whatever point of view we consider the infliction of penalty as a mean of restricting the
intercourse of Sentiment, or of preventing the
progress of Falsehood, we shall find it diametrically repugnant to just and rational principles.*

* The Act of the State of Virginia for establishing Religious Freedom, passed in 1786, though confined to Theological subjects, is equally applicable to Political. It contains a summary of incontrovertible
reasoning in favor of the Liberty of Enquiry, from which the following
remarks are extracted :—" To suffer the Civil Magistrate to intrude his
powers into the field of Opinion, and to restrain the profession or propagation of principles on supposition of their ill tendency, is a dangerous fallacy, which at once destroys all (religious) liberty : because he
being, of course, judge of that tendency, will make his opinions the rule
of judgment ; and approve or condemn the sentiments of others, only as

We have not yet sufficiently considered the
subject upon one of its most important and in-
Inter-   teresting grounds.   An unrestricted investiga-
course of
opinion tion of the conduct of Magistrates, is not only
the only
preserva- a necessary preventative of the encroachments
tive of Li-
berty.   of Ambition, but it is also the only preservative
of Public Liberty which can be resorted to
without endangering the tranquility of a State.
It will ever be found impossible in practice to
admit the interference of Government for the
restriction of Public Opinion, without destroying the efficiency, or enfeebling the operation
of the censorial powers of Society.

Two opposite and formidable evils are always
to be sedulously avoided : first, the Extension
of Prerogative beyond its beneficial or constitutional limits ; and, secondly, the unsalutary Re-
laxation of Political Authority and Discipline.
With respect to the latter evil, there is very little danger of its ever becoming realized.   The
vigilant superintendance of regular Government,
a disciplined body, constantly jealous of the di-
minution of its powers, and always active and

---

they shall square with or differ from his own.   It is time enough for the
rightful purposes of Civil Government for its officers to interfere when
principles break out into overt acts against Peace and Good Order.   And,
finally, that Truth is great, and will prevail, if left to herself; that she
is the proper and sufficient antagonist to Error ; and has nothing to fear
from the conflict, unless by human interposition disarmed of her natural
weapons, Free Argument and Debate : errors ceasing to be dangerous
when it is permitted freely to contradict them,"

in motion, is a sufficient pledge for the duration _{CHAP.}
and exercise of political authority.

All Governments have an inevitable tendency to aspire. The passion for extending Prerogative is ever active and alive. It is, therefore,
indispensable to the preservation of the constitutional equipoise of Power, that such tendency
should be perpetually balanced by a principle
not only vigorous but independent. It should
always be remembered, that Government possesses an evident advantage and superiority over
every species of opposition ; it is a regular, disciplined, and organized corps ; its moral and
physical energies are concentrated and combined ; it is capable of steady premeditation and
continual design ; it never loses sight of its object : but, with undeviating constancy, pursues
its plans through the mazes of events, and in
the midst of every obstacle. It is equally qualified to contrive and to execute : It perpetually
exists, and slumbers not. Let it be added, it
directs and commands all the resources of a
State. Unless, therefore, some vigilant, powerful, and independent corrective is retained by
Society, nothing can prevent its becoming the
devoted victim of Despotism.

Public Opinion is the only check which can
be judiciously opposed to the encroachments of
Prerogative. All other resistance would not

CHAP.
XII. only be ineffectual and perilous, but subversive
of every valuable principle of the social state.
Disorder and Violence should be severely dis-
countenanced by every enlightened advocate of
Freedom. Let us fondly anticipate the gradual
improvement of Civil Institution from the unrestricted progress of Reason : for we have every thing to dread from the licentious and un-
bridled intemperance of Passion.

Should Public Opinion should not only remain un-
be inde-
pendent. connected with Civil Authority, but be rendered superior to its controul. As the guardian of
Public Liberty it will lose its powers and its usefulness the moment it is rendered dependent
upon the Government. The stream must flow
in the direction to which it naturally inclines,
and not be diverted by subtlety or force. No
superintendance should be introduced, except
what is exercised by the percipient faculties of
Danger of Society. Coercion will stamp an awe upon the
investing mind which will infallibly destroy the freedom
Govern-
ment with of Public Opinion. However innocent or cor-
means to
controul it rect may be our sentiments, we shall always remain uncertain with respect to the verdict to be
pronounced upon them ; we shall perpetually
distrust the impartiality or discernment of the
tribunal before which we are liable to be summoned. The consequences of mistake will be
so fatal and destructive, that we shall be driven
to the pernicious alternative of silence and inex-

ertion. The history of prosecutions for libel ^{Chap.}
XII.
will constantly furnish us with the lesson, That
Governments are impatient of contradiction;
that they are not so zealous to punish Falsehood
from an enlightened and disinterested attachment to Justice, as they are ready to smother
opinions that are unfavorable to their designs.
The infliction of Penalty, instead of being a
wholesome corrective of Falsehood, will be perpetually abused to answer the purposes of Animosity, Oppression, and Ambition. It will infallibly destroy that censorial jurisdiction of Society which is the only salutary preservative of
Public Liberty and Justice.

Previous to dismissing the present branch of Objection
from the
necessary
secrecy of
particular
transac-
tions.
enquiry, it may be of importance to anticipate
an objection which arises from the necessary secrecy of particular measures of Government.
It is true, as a general position, that publicity
should constitute an essential characteristic of
political transactions: but in the present state
of Civil Society this rule is liable to some exception. There are certain measures which cannot
be made public without evident disadvantage,
and exposure to the hazard of defeat.

Such exception is confined within extremely Answer.
narrow bounds. It will principally relate to
subjects of extraordinary occurrence. We may

instance the pre-determined operations of a campaign, and the instructions which are given to public ambassadors ; and perhaps it will be difficult to imagine another parallel case. It is undoubtedly proper that our military plans, the destination of our fleets, or the projected enterprises of our armies, should be cautiously concealed from the knowledge of an enemy : it is equally important in negociation that the opposite cabinet should remain profoundly ignorant of the extent of concession we had determined to make. Let us now examine how far such considerations will affect the doctrines that have hitherto been maintained.

It is readily admitted that Secrecy in such cases should be carefully observed so long as Concealment is necessary to ensure the success of the negociation or enterprize. At the moment when Concealment ceases to be essential, it becomes the duty of Government to submit the propriety of its conduct to public investigation. But in the mean-while, it will be contended, that its proceedings will be liable to misrepresentation. To this let it be answered,

In the first place, a community whose discernment is strengthened by the habits of political discussion will find no difficulty in perceiving the necessity of Secrecy in such particular instances. If it is not known that a military enterprize is contemplated, or that a negociation is depending, it is plain that they cannot become the subjects of enquiry or conversation : but if it has been vaguely reported, or indefinitely published, that an armament is to be employed, or a treaty concluded; if the people have witnessed warlike preparations, or become informed of the appointment of ambassadors, they will patiently await the developement of the plot. Misrepresentation upon those occasions would not be accompanied with any serious mischief. It would not acquire numerous partizans, because it would be perfectly understood that it is necessarily derived from the idle speculations of conjecture. If any of the confidants of Government should have betrayed the secret, the story, like every other, must derive its credit from the weight of testimony.

Secondly, Government should in such cases rest with security upon its general reputation of integrity and veracity. If it has been accustomed to an ample and faithful publication of its transactions with respect to other concerns, it will unquestionably establish its character of patriotism and rectitude, and attach to itself the confidence of the People, whenever that confidence in secret transactions is indispensible.

Thirdly, It is an incontrovertible position, That the punishment of Truth is incompatible

with the dictates of Political Justice. Now it
is evident, that, while those transactions are
enveloped in secrecy, it is impossible to determine whether any assertion concerning them is
in reality true or unfounded. It is, therefore,
improper that such assertion should be made
the subject of judicial decision. It is equally
improper that any punishment should become
inflicted. The public have no method of ascertaining the propriety or justice of the sentence.
Such prosecutions should not be tolerated, because their abuses are incapable of detection :
but the moment those transactions become de-
veloped, and unfolded in detail, the effect of
Misrepresentation vanishes like a meteor, and
Coercion is consequently rendered useless and
unnecessary..

Further
remarks.
There is no view in which we can contemplate the system of Restriction, without perceiving its injustice and deformity. It can never be necessary to preserve the order and tranquility of Society, but is perpetually liable to
the most pernicious prostitution. It can never
be essential to the security of beneficial institutions, but may be rendered an engine of the
most atrocious oppression when guided by the
hand of Despotism. Public Opinion is the vital
principle of Civil Society : the healthful existence of a state requires that it should always
possess a considerable latitude and extensive

sphere of operation, and that it should never be Chap.
XII.
approached without the utmost deference and
circumspection.   To invest the public magistrate with the power of restricting Opinion,
would be to trust the progress of Information to
the mercy and pleasure of a Government ! More
formidable dangers are justly to be apprehended
from arming the constituted organs of Authority
with a power to arrest the career of Human Intellect, than from all the evils attributable to
Licentiousness.   Shall a vicious administration
be permitted to shelter itself by the tyrannical
severity of its edicts, or fortify its authority by
the inhuman cruelty of its penal code ? Shall it
erect the pallisades of Criminal Jurisprudence
to prevent the rude approach of independent
Investigation ? Shall statutes be enacted to render Enquiry criminal, and laws be enforced to
metamorphose Reflection into Treason or Sedition ? What reasoner will pretend to assert the
absolute infallibility of Government, or maintain
that every act of administration must necessarily
be stamped with the features of Perfection ? If
a community may sometimes err in the formation of their sentiments, Governments will not
less frequently oppress the people from premeditated design.   The censorial jurisdiction of
Society is the only safe and wholesome guardian
of Public Liberty.   It can exercise its beneficial province no longer than while it retains
an absolute independence.   As far as conside-

CHAP.
XII. rations of danger are implicated in the discussion, the argument unequivocally terminates
in favor of the most unbounded latitude of Investigation.

CHAPTER XIII.

The Freedom of Investigation considered as a Preventative of Revolution.

Horrors of Revolution—Lead to a prejudicial conclusion—Progress of Reason the most effectual preventative—Vindication of the Advocate of Liberty.

In treating the subject upon general Chap.
XIII. grounds, and before we proceed to its examination with relation to particular systems of political institution, it yet remains to be considered in a truly interesting and serious point of view. There is still a light in which the picture can become presented, which cannot fail to awaken the solicitude of Mind, and engage the most fervent sensibilities of the Heart.

To destroy the empire of Despotism, and to meliorate its political condition, Society possesses but two remedies : it must either resort to Revolution, or trust to the progressive illumination of the general understanding. The former is desperate, calamitous, and of uncertain issue : the latter, though gradual, and almost imperceptible, is constant, uniform, and steady in its operations. By appreciating the concomitant horrors and miseries of Revolution, we shall unavoidably become more deeply interested in the salutary progression of Knowledge.

Horrors of Revolution.

Whatever may be the ultimate termination of sudden revolutions in the institutions of a state, in their origin and progress they are infallibly accompanied with the most formidable and tremendous calamities. Hasty transitions are invariably violent : they proceed from the irregular effusions of Passion, Animosity, and Vengeance, rather than from the calm and benevolent decisions of rational and independent Reflection. Convulsion is the natural element of the turbulent, the factious, and the unprincipled : it is too stormy and impetuous for the peaceful, salutary, and cautious progression of Truth. Hence it follows, that the most experienced and enlightened ornaments of Society are forcibly obtruded from the sphere into which their experience and their virtues entitled them to move. The political barque at once becomes plunged into the eventful crisis of Mutiny and Tempest ; and, while the horizon becomes ob-

scured with impenetrable darkness—while lightning darts and thunder roars—in the midst of
general perturbation and universal convulsion,
some rash, impatient, and ignorantly adventurous hand, will violently grasp the helm, and
guide the vessel to destruction.

The period of violent Revolution is ever a
period of the most complicated tyranny. Its
code is Ferocity, its constitution is Proscription,
and its edicts are written in blood.   Is that a
time of Liberty ? or can it be a moment pregnant with improvement, when the fruits of honest industry are tortured from our possession ;
when every door in Civil Society is suddenly
projected from its hinges ; and every peaceable
asylum, and every sacred temple of Retirement,
open to the entrance of a sanguinary and enfuri-
ate mob ? There is not the tyranny of Institution,
because no legitimate institution exists.   It is
not the despotism of a tyrant, from whose cruelty we can flee, or whose premeditated vengeance we can cautiously elude : the calamity
rushes in upon us at our most unguarded mo-
ments ; we feel the dagger in our expiring hearts
without time to explain or to prepare—without
an instant for expostulation.   If we are permitted the hallowed rites of sepulture, rather for
the benefit of the living than of the dead, with
our gore-streaming vestments around us we de-

scend into our silent tombs, unsanctified, " un-
anointed, unanealed." There is neither mercy
nor atonement : we fall the sudden, lifeless victims of Vengeance, without recognizing the as-
sassin who strikes the deadly blow. In such
terrible conjunctures of moral disorganization
and social convulsion, there is no Justice, no
Virtue, and no Principle ; nothing is respected,
consecrated, or secured ; Confidence and Friend-
ship are extirpated ; Fear is seated in every bosom ; Distrust and Terror distort and brutalize
the features of every countenance. Where shall
we search for sincerity, candour, and manly fortitude, when suspicion lurks in every heart, and
the tongue no longer speaks ingenuously whatever the understanding conceives ? Despotism
is a PROTEUS, that can assume every disguise,
and present itself in every variety of shape. With
disordered tresses, starting eyes, and frantic
mien, it can personate the Furies, and call itself by the name of Revolution and Anarchy.
With equal facility it can ornament itself with
diamonds, and become decorated with the sceptre and the imperial purple. Uniform in cruelty, and constant in its vengeance, still it grasps
the murdering sword, or administers the deadly
poison. I call upon the Philosopher and Moralist, I conjure the Practical Magistrate, at-
tentively to reflect upon the means for the prevention of such direful calamities.

A consideration of the evils necessarily attendant upon violent convulsions in Society, has, in
most instances, occasioned an impolitic and
irrational conclusion. Men, by no means con-
temptible in understanding, or deficient in ac-
quirement, have imbibed an attachment to the
errors and prejudices of existing institutions,
from an apprehension that innovation is inseparably accompanied with dreadful and sanguinary consequences. The preceding picture is only appropriate to those premature and convulsive
Revolutions which sooner or later are the inevitable result of Despotism. It is far from being
questioned that in a period of violent Revolution
neither Property, Liberty, or Life are deposited
in the sanctuary of Virtue, or placed in the as-
sylum of Security. It is further admitted, that
in most cases the ultimate effect and termination of a state of Revolution is a matter of extreme perplexity and incertitude. There is,
perhaps, as great a probability that one Despotism may be destroyed only for the purpose of
giving place to another, as that the empire of
free and rational Government will succeed to
the deposition of a former tyrant. The reign of
Disorder is not adapted to continued or permanent existence. Society soon becomes exhaust-
ed by violent and convulsive struggle. Para-
lized by the impetuosity of Effort, it will sink
into the arms of some powerful and fortunate
Usurper. In those Revolutions its physical

force is not directed by its moral powers : it is
rather propelled by the sudden ebullitions of
Passion, than guided by the regular and sober
dictates of Judicious Discernment. Passion is
incapable of lengthy duration : it is a self-mur-
derer, which becomes the speedy victim of its
own impolitic violence. It will be found upon
examination that the most effectual method of
preventing Revolutions, is to destroy the incentives by which they are ordinarily created. The
most certain mean to avoid Convulsions, is to
guard against the abuses by which they are usually provoked.

Touch not that spring in human Society
which directs, propels, and governs its regular
movements. Lay not the iron hand of Power
on that elastic principle, upon the animated existence of which depends the vitality of the
state. What victim resigns its breath without a
struggle ? What is it that dies without experi-
encing a previous convulsion ? Who can foretell
the consequences which may arise from the impolitic exercise of Civil Authority ? The history
of mankind, so pregnant with vicissitudes, must
convince us that Revolutions, and intestine
commotions, have invariably proceeded from
the Abuse of Power. Dreadful as is their operation, they are scarcely more deprecable than
the lifeless slumber of Despotism.

It is impossible that Society should remain Chap. XIII. forever stationary. Perhaps its constant progression in improvement has now become inevitable. From the experience of former ages in affairs of Government, it would be hazardous exclusively to reason. The state of mankind in the ages that have passed was different from that in which they are placed at present. Greece and Rome are usually denominated enlightened countries : but in those celebrated communities Knowledge was monopolized, and confined to the possession of a few. The means of its acquisition were trivial ; those of its preservation slender. If books were written, they could not be generally circulated : the multiplication of copies was scantily effected by the tedious and laborious industry of manual penmanship ; and they were exclusively devoted to the perusal of the wealthy and the scientific. The unenlightened multitude were more easily deluded and governed, because it was their perpetual destiny to remain uninstructed. No periodical publications, no friendly volumes of Truth, were dedicated to their instruction, or ushered into the world for general benefit. Who cannot perceive that the invention of Printing has fixed the date of a most remarkable æra in the general history of Mankind ?

These considerations cannot be pronounced a digression from the subject principally in view :

Progress of reason the most effectual preventative.

CHAP.
XIII. for, by appreciating the horrors of a state of Revolution, the mind becomes more fervently attached to that excellent mean of prevention
which supercedes its necessity, and points to
the progressive melioration of Society, by a
hand unstained with blood. The influence of
the press upon opinions, manners, and government, is a subject which will presently be submitted to attention. In proportion as our topic
is extensive, it demands the invigorated energy
of Investigation : but previous to the termination of the present Chapter, let us endeavour to
rescue the advocates of Political Reformation
from an imputation with which they have been
unjustly stigmatized.

Vindica-
tion of the   It is a prejudice not unfrequently entertained,
advocates that the advocates of Public Liberty are restless,
of liberty.
turbulent, and seditious ; perpetually addicted
to the pursuit of novelty, and ever watchful for
the opportunity of Revolution. To remove a
prejudice, at once so fatal and delusive, is a
duty equally owing to the safety of the Government, and the permanent welfare of the People.
Such an opinion may excite the apprehensions
of administration, and lead them to the adoption of measures creative of discontent, and liable to terminate in the very evils they are studi-
ous to avoid ; it may influence the weak, the
timid, and the affluent, and induce them to oppose the benevolent efforts of Melioration di-

rected to the general benefit. Philosophical _{CHAP.} _{XIII.}
Reformation is not a crude and visionary pro-
jector: Rashness is not her attribute, nor physical Force her weapon. Her province is to enlighten Society by candid and argumentative
addresses to the understanding. She is the benefactor of the human race, imbued with wisdom, moderation, and clemency ; and not " the
destroying Angel," who would sacrifice one generation from uncertain prospects of benefit to
the next. Her genuine task is to preserve the
lives of millions, to respect the private posses-
sions of the people, and forbid the sanguinary
streams to flow. Her constant solicitude is not
to invite mankind to assemble amid the ferocious din of arms, but in the peaceful temple of
Reason and Reflection.

We have already seen that the security of Government and the conservation of Public Liberty
rest upon the same common basis, Public Opinion. Those very sentiments of political rectitude, which render a community solicitous for
the preservation of every essential right, will infallibly deter them from resorting to revolution-
ary measures for the redress of public grievances. It is, therefore, more dangerous for Government to risque the destruction of that general mass of information which sustains the morals
of Society, than to permit the most industrious
activity and unbounded latitude of Investiga-

tion. If any case can possibly occur, which can render the violence of Revolution expedient, it must be when all hope of redress from any other remedy has completely vanished ; it must be when the authority of Government debars that mutual intercourse and communication of Opinion which is essential to general knowledge and improvement. Of every possible mode of Despotism, there is none so pernicious, none from which the mind of man shrinks back with greater horror, than that which brutalizes his moral and percipient faculties, and deprives him of the inestimable property of an Intelligent Being, Freedom of Speech and Opinion. The habitude of reasoning, and the liberty of communicating our sentiments, are friendly alike to the rights of Society and to the wholesome authority of Government. Licentiousness is an evil infinitely less formidable than Restriction.

CHAPTER XIV.

𝕮𝖍𝖊 𝖕𝖗𝖊𝖈𝖊𝖉𝖎𝖓𝖌 𝖘𝖚𝖇𝖏𝖊𝖈𝖙𝖘 𝖈𝖔𝖓𝖘𝖎𝖉𝖊𝖗𝖊𝖉 𝖜𝖎𝖙𝖍 𝖗𝖊𝖑𝖆𝖙𝖎𝖔𝖓 𝖙𝖔 𝕽𝖊𝖕𝖗𝖊𝖘𝖊𝖓-
𝖙𝖆𝖙𝖎𝖛𝖊 𝕲𝖔𝖛𝖊𝖗𝖓𝖒𝖊𝖓𝖙𝖘.

Theory of Representation—Limitation of the
Elective Privilege——Vindicated——Opposed—
Question undecided—Of Property—Investiga-
tion essential—As it respects the Candidate—
As it respects the Elector—Restriction unsalu-
tary and repugnant.

Thus far the subject has been examined upon general and independent grounds.
The doctrine of the preceding chapters is unconnected with any particular form of civil institution. We become furnished with an additional field of argument when it is considered
with relation to the theory of Representative
Systems.

CHAP.
XIV.   The Society which is wholly erected upon the
basis of Representation is undoubtedly most
Theory of congenial to the nature and moral constitution
Represen-
tation.   of man.   It embraces the sound position, That
the exclusive object of Civil Government is to
promote the general benefit ; and it constantly
exhibits the perfect equality of political rights.
No hereditary aristocracy usurps the powers of
the state ; no privileged orders are supported at
the expence of the people ;   and no exclusive
immunities are monopolized by the partially distinguished few.   Our understanding is not in-
sulted by the insignificant parade of empty and
unmeaning titles :   but (except what is descrip-
tive of substantial office) the general name of *Citizen*, which expresses our relation to the community, is the only appellation of the social
state.

Limita-   It has, however, been the policy of most
tion of the
Elective Governments, which have either wholly or in
Privilege.
part been founded upon the representative system, in some measure to limit the operation of
the principle of Representation, by requiring
certain qualifications to be possessed, not only
by the candidate of office, but also by those who
claim a voice in his election.   Those qualifications most usually consist in the possession of
property.   It may be a matter of useful speculation to examine the reasoning in favor of such

limitation, and the arguments by which it may become opposed.

In support of such limitation it may be urged, with considerable force, that the interest of Society is a consideration to which every other principle must bend; and that the public good requires that no man should possess a voice in the general councils unless his situation is independent. It is true, indeed, that poverty should be viewed as a misfortune, and not considered as a crime : but that he who is exposed to penury will be perpetually subjected to the influence, and implicitly devoted to the views, of the rich ; that the opposers of such limitation entirely mistake the means of promoting the object they profess to have in view ; for that by furnishing the affluent with an opportunity to render those who are dependent upon their favor, and exposed to the temptation of their bribes, the tools and instruments of their ambition, instead of promoting, they would effectually destroy the substantial equality of political rights.

In addition to this, it is further maintained, That the welfare of Society requires every active citizen to be deeply interested in the prosperity of the state : he should feel that he has something valuable at stake ; something that may operate as a perpetual pledge to ensure his political integrity. He who possesses a property

CHAP.
XIV.

in the soil may be considered as a permanent member of Society ; his citizenship is established upon a solid and durable foundation : but he who has little to lose will seldom be animated by an ardent solicitude for the public prosperity. The individual who is possessed of property, will act with principle and independence : but the child of Poverty is a feather that may be wafted by the lightest breeze.

Opposed.

On the other hand it may be contended that it is an essential political principle, That all who are bound by the laws should possess an equal share in their formation ; that the individual who is not blessed with the perishable goods of Fortune has nevertheless the more estimable treasures of Liberty and Life : shall these become subjected to the authority of institutions, in the establishment of which their possessor has no agency ? Shall the individual who is poor be taught to feel that he is not a citizen ? If he has no interest at stake, with what countenance can he be called upon to fight the battles of that which cannot be considered as his country ? Vicissitude is an imperious law of mortals, and the clouds of Misfortune are suspended over every Son of Humanity. He who is the boasted proprietor of wealth and independence to-day, may be stripped of the fleeting gifts of PLUTUS by the unforeseen events of to-morrow.

It may further be objected, That the Aristo- _CH_AP.
cracy of Wealth exerts a pernicious empire over XIV.
Manners and Morals ; that the distinction Aristo-
which it creates is extremely unfavorable to the Wealth.
progress and the practice of Virtue ; that the
true use of property becomes perverted from
that end for which it was originally designed ;
that riches are not coveted for the valuable and
virtuous enjoyment which they are enabled to
bestow, but for the pernicious ostentation and
influence which they cherish ; that Society constantly impresses the baneful lesson, " Exert all
the powers you possess for the attainment of af-
fluence, for without this you can never become
respectable or happy :

" ———— Quærenda PECUNIA primum
" Virtus post nummos :"

That neither Talents nor Virtue enforce our esteem unless they are united with the possession
of Wealth ; and that accordingly Avarice has
become the predominant passion of Society, and
Fraud and Peculation crimes of continual recurrence : That Property will always command a
sufficient degree of influence, without being
rendered the subject of exclusive political privileges ; and that every limitation of the representative principle is not only unjust, but highly
pernicious.

Such are some of the principal considerations
involved in the discussion of that interesting
question. We shall not at present venture to
decide to what determination the weight of argument will direct. With regard to this, as
well as every other subject, the welfare of Society should constitute the exclusive standard of
decision. Let it, however, be observed, that
the Equalization of Property, however favorite
an object it may be in Utopian theories, is perhaps altogether incapable of becoming realized
in practice. If it was possible to establish the
most perfect equality at one moment, it would
instantly become destroyed by the avarice of
one and the prodigality of another. Agrarian
laws are constantly pernicious ; and the interference of Government upon such occasions
would amount to the most atrocious and deprecable tyranny. Let Property pursue its own
level, and ebb, and flow, and fluctuate with
the vicissitudes of life.

These considerations, though they belong to
the Representative System, are mentioned inci-
dentally, and do not materially affect the principal doctrines of this Chapter : for the man
who is possessed of property and the elective
privilege to-day, may lose them, and he who
has them not may acquire them on the mor-
row.

Let us, then, proceed to examine the right of Chap. XIV. Political Investigation as it particularly relates to the theory of Representative Government. Investigation essential to the Representative theory. Whether such system of political institution is pure and unmixed, or whether it is restricted and modified, it is in either case a fundamental position, That public offices are conferred by the suffrages of Society ; and that every individual either actually has, or may acquire, a right to be elected, as well as a voice in elections.

In the first place, therefore, every member of As it respects the Elected. a Representative Commonwealth either is or may become eligible to be invested with public offices. It is for that reason absolutely indispensible to the existence of such system that each individual should be furnished with all the means of obtaining political information, and be permitted to exercise his faculties in the pursuit of such knowledge without interruption or restraint. The idea of Secrecy is peculiarly repugnant to the theory of Representative Institution, except in those solitary instances which render temporary concealment necessary. So far from discouraging Enquiry, it is the genuine spirit of such system to stimulate the mind to enterprize, awaken emulation, and point to the honorable rewards of superior excellence and talents. Society should constitute an University of Politics, open to the instruction of each of its members. In this extensive school each indi-

CHAP.
XIV.

vidual who will exert the powers of his mind, ought to be taught not only the general principles of political morality, but also the particular and local interests of the state.

As it respects the Elector.

Secondly, The liberty of investigation is equally indispensible to the judicious exercise of the elective right. It is to be presumed that the elector, who prefers between contending candidates, decides from the influence of reasons which are present to his understanding. He is supposed to assume the province of a judge with respect to their principles, talents, and political acquirements. Now, to enable one man to decide upon the qualifications of another, it is necessary that he should be conversant with that branch of knowledge which respects those qualifications. It is therefore necessary, in the discharge of such important duty, that the elector should be enabled to exercise every means of information. In proportion as a community is habituated to political discussion, its discernment will be rendered accurate and comprehensive ; it will acquire the faculty of distinguishing merit ; and the Representative form of Government will more nearly approach perfection than any other system, because Wisdom and Virtue will acquire the offices of state.

Thirdly, It is to be observed, That the Representative System unavoidably implics an ab-

solute right to investigate the conduct of all pub- CHAP.
lic officers. And here let Attention be directed XIV.
to a most important consideration, which places such system in an amiable and interesting
light, and confers upon it a pre-eminent superiority over any other. While every other form
of civil government is totally destitute of any regular remedy to redress the encroachments of
Power, the system of Representation possesses
an efficacious corrective inseparably entwined
around the heart of its constitution. In monarchies and hereditary establishments a dreadful
alternative is presented to our choice : we must
either tamely submit to accumulated wrongs, or
by resistance disorganize and convulse the social frame. But in elective governments the remedy is regular, peaceful, and of constant periodical recurrence. The magistrate whose conduct has been injurious may be displaced, and
his seat bestowed upon a more upright and patriotic successor. Let, then, the advocate of
Freedom be enjoined to abstain from violence ;
let him carefully avoid every act of disorder ;
let his conduct exhibit an exemplary submission
to the laws ; and let the public be taught to
cherish and esteem the elective privilege, as the
only safe and constitutional mean of redress.

But it is plain that such remedy would be
feeble and inactive unless associated with its

correspondent right of enquiry into the conduct of public officers. Society, as the constituent body, must determine whether they are entitled to a continuance of confidence ; and whether the general welfare requires that they shall be re-elected or displaced. Every elector, therefore, must be permitted to canvass the conduct of public officers with unshaken firmness and independence.

For this purpose it is indispensibly requisite that political measures should be published in circumstantial detail, and also that Investigation should remain entirely unrestricted. It is necessary that the public should be placed in the possession of events, and also of the reasoning and incentives with which they are connected. It is equally necessary that their decision should be rendered independent of controul. Surely it would be presumptuous in the public officer to tell his constituent, " My elevation is dependent upon the tenure of your pleasure ; you possess the constitutional right to displace me : but I will not permit you to exercise that pleasure, or you shall only exercise it in such manner as I think proper to prescribe."

Fourthly, It is to be observed that the investigation of Conduct must inevitably lead to the investigation of Character. Every man who becomes a candidate for office voluntarily submits

his reputation to the ordeal of Public Examination. Surely, if my suffrage is requested in favor of any individual, it is my duty to enquire
what are his qualifications? What his morals?
Is he entitled to public confidence? What are
his pretensions to the virtue of Integrity? If Pericles, who has already been appointed to office, should become a candidate for re-election,
how is it possible that I can enter into an examination of his conduct, and yet abstain from
an investigation of his character? Let me be
informed of the substantial reason why I should
abstain? If his conduct is too frail to admit the
contact of enquiry, what are his pretensions to
public promotion? If it is not feeble, why
should he shrink from the touchstone of Investigation? What is Character? What are the evidences upon which it is founded? and what are
the ideas associated with that term? The general tenor of our conduct has been useful and
upright; we have uniformly manifested that
our actions proceed from honest intentions.
From such general train of procedure Character
is derived. Character and general Conduct are,
therefore, correlative. An examination of the
one implies an examination of the other.

Lastly, the idea of Restriction is peculiarly Restrictions un-
salutary
and re-
pugnant.
repugnant to the theory of Representation. It
is not to be expected that the investigation of
public character, a right of such continual re-

currence, will be altogether unaccompanied
with mistake ; perhaps it will be frequently attended even with intentional misrepresentation :
but what tribunal shall decide upon that point?
Public prosecutions in such cases will be always
liable to abuse : they will infallibly be made a
tremendous weapon in the hands of the officers
of state to oppress and intimidate the people.
Individuals concerned in administration will be
influenced by a common spirit to render themselves inviolable ; and, until Patriotism becomes
more generally connected with Authority than
it ever has been, they will gladly maintain a
CERBERUS at the doors of the council chamber
to prevent the rude and unbidden approach of
Scrutiny.

It is better to submit to a partial evil, than
by injudicious violence incur a more extensive
calamity. Governments have not hitherto reposed sufficient confidence in Truth : they have
too uniformly endeavoured to combat Moral
Imperfection with Physical Force. If men are
subject to punishment on account of their errors,
they will be enfeebled with a degree of timidity
and distrust which will impair the activity of
the Representative System. The frequency of
prosecutions in such cases will undermine the
only remedy we possess against the misconduct
of our representatives. It would be even better
that a public officer should sustain an inconve-

nience, than a community be inspired with ter- ror. ● But there will be ample means of redress without resorting to criminal prosecutions. The publication of Truth will be sufficient to remove any unfounded stigma ; and if the representative conceives that he has sustained a personal injury, let him resort to the civil judicature. We are to consider that the elective franchise is the only constitutional corrective of abuses ; and that it will be enfeebled by any power which paralizes the Liberty of Investigation. It is far better to err on the side of Latitude than on that of Restraint. Every man should be suffered to approach that inviolable palladium with a temper ardent, and a mind unterrified. Restraint is always liable to be converted into an engine of Oppression : it will constantly damp the energy of Public Spirit, and awe the timid and the irresolute into an abdication of their rights. The healthful vigour of the Representative System requires that the elective privilege, together with its correspondent rights, should be maintained in a state of incessant activity and independence. If any temporary evils do arise from Licentiousness, it is better to trust to the soundness of the political constitution than to tamper with the vital principles of the state.

CHAPTER XV.

𝕮𝖍𝖊 𝖘𝖆𝖒𝖊 𝖘𝖚𝖇𝖏𝖊𝖈𝖙𝖘 𝖈𝖔𝖓𝖘𝖎𝖉𝖊𝖗𝖊𝖉 𝖜𝖎𝖙𝖍 𝖗𝖊𝖑𝖆𝖙𝖎𝖔𝖓 𝖙𝖔 𝖙𝖍𝖊 𝕮𝖔𝖓𝖘𝖙𝖎𝖙𝖚𝖙𝖎𝖔𝖓
𝖔𝖋 𝖙𝖍𝖊 𝖀𝖓𝖎𝖙𝖊𝖉 𝕾𝖙𝖆𝖙𝖊𝖘.

Historical outlines of the confederation—Summary of the legislative powers of Congress—Reasoning from such premises—Summary of judicial powers—Reasoning therefrom.

W E shall now attempt to examine Chap. the subject with more immediate relation to the XV. Constitution of the United States.

Our Government is entirely founded in the System of Representation. The doctrines of the preceding Chapter, are therefore particularly applicable thereto.

Two important and interesting questions are here presented to our attention : the first, Whether Congress possesses legislative authority with

respect to libels ? The second, Whether the judiciary of the United States have jurisdiction in
such cases.   These questions must be determined by the Record of the Constitution.

In the interpretation of that instrument, we
shall derive considerable assistance from a previous review of our political origin and history,
and of the spirit and nature of our fœderate system.

Historical
outlines of
the Con-
federation.
A number of distinct Colonies possessed of
Territory in point of situation approximate and
compact, inhabited by men speaking a common
language, governed by similar laws, and influenced by the same manners.   Men who were
accustomed to the continual reciprocity of intercourse, and mostly connected by the powerful ties of national ancestry, during a long succession of years, are the duteous and submissive
dependents of a distant, ambitious, and enter-
prizing Kingdom.   The jealousy or rapacity of
the imperial State creates a system of oppression,
and rather accelerates than produces a separa-
tion which was one day unavoidable.

Possessed of an unity of interest, and conscious of the necessity of associating their means of
defence, the American Colonies become united
by a compact of Confederation.   Finding that
their remonstrances are treated with unmerited

contempt, and that every prospect of conciliation had vanished. In a general Congress of those Colonies, each of them, by the united voice of all, is declared to be a free and independent State. And when at length their arms became crowned with victory and success, such memorable declaration was sanctioned and confirmed by the definitive treaty of Peace.

The same urgent considerations which dictated an union of the Colonies must ever continue to cherish an union of the States. The contending passions and ambition of separate Governments, the mutual jealousy and discordant interests of so many rival powers, would inevitably expose us to a renewal of those dreadful scenes of hostility which have desolated the fertile plains of Europe, and drenched them with the blood of countless millions. Upon the restoration of peace we became taught by experience to discover the feebleness and inefficiency of our former Articles of Confederation, and were finally led to the adoption of our present general Constitution.

This Constitution must be considered in a two-fold point of view. First, as a compact of union between the States; and second, as the instrument which creates, defines, and limits the powers of the Government.

CHAP.
XV.   The term "*Federal*," which is usually and
properly applied to our general Constitution, is
derived from the latin "*Fœdus*," signifying a
league.   It implies that each of the contracting
States retains its existence and its sovereignty,
subject to the limitations imposed by the compact of Confederation, and is evidently distinguishable from Consolidation, which would suppose that the separate existence of each State
was lost in the general body.

The powers which are usually associated with
the idea of sovereignty are therefore divided.
Some are conferred upon the general Government, and others are retained by the State.
"The powers not delegated to the United States
by the Constitution, nor prohibited by it to the
States, are reserved to the States respectively or
to the people."

Each of the States retains its separate Legislature, and a limited or qualified sovereignty.
Their respective governments act without controul in their spheres, and move independently
within their orbits.*

---

* With honest enthusiasm, with patriotic exultation we may congra-
tulate each other on the peculiar excellence of our Political System.   It
has been a dogma more generally credited than accurately examined,
that Republican Governments are not suited to extensive territory or
numerous population.   This assertion cannot extend to a *Representative*
much less to a *Fœderate Republic*.   It is scarcely possible that any system should unite *Stability* with the *Spirit of Freedom* in a greater degree
than the Government of the United States.

The Government of the United States is a _{Chap.} XV. limited system. It was instituted for specific and particular purposes. The objects it embraces are such as relate to the general interests of

Speaking of a Confederate Republic the celebrated MONTESQUIEU observes, " A Republic of this kind, able to withstand an external force, may support itself without any internal corruption ; the form of this Society prevents all manner of inconveniences."

" If a single member should attempt to usurp the supreme power he could not be supposed to have an equal authority and credit in all the Confederate States. Were he to have too great an influence over one, this would alarm the rest ; were he to subdue a part, that which would still remain free might oppose him with forces independent of those which he had usurped, and overpower him before he could be settled in his usurpation."

" Should a popular insurrection happen in one of the Confederate States the others are able to quell it. Should abuses creep into one part, they are reformed by those that remain sound. The state may be destroyed on one side, and not on the other ; the confederacy may be dissolved, and the confederates preserve their sovereignty."

" As this Government is composed of petty Republics, it enjoys the internal happiness of each ; and with regard to its external situation, by means of the association it possesses all the advantages of large Monarchies."

MONTESQUIEU further observes, that the Governments of the respective States should be similar. This advantage is eminently possessed by our confederacy.

Let it be observed, that the mutability of a Republic one and indivisible cannot be charged to a Confederate Republic.

The powers of a Federal Government should be definite and precise ; they should be such as to ensure respect, yet not to enable it to act the tyrant. Our own system appears to possess the happy medium. If any thing is wanting it is something that will explain with more precision the extent of its powers.

Chap.
XV.

the Confederacy.   Those of domestic or interior concern belong to the legislatures of the respective States.   When we apply the epithet *general* to the Government of the United States, the expression alludes to the *relation* in which it stands, and not to the *universality* of its authority.

The objects of federal jurisdiction are specifically defined.   The powers vested in the general Government are such as are expressly and particularly granted by the Constitution, or such as flow in obvious and necessary consequence from the authorities which are thus expressly conferred.

Powers claimed by implication should be such as follow from evident and necessary construction, and not in consequence of distant or conjectural interpretation.   Much latitude cannot be admitted upon the occasion without endangering Public Liberty and destroying the symmetry of our Political System.

I.   *Does Congress possess Legislative Authority in cases of Libel ?*

It is well that neither of our parties are entrusted with the formation of a Constitution.   The Jealousy of the one would render it too lax, the Spirit of the other too luxuriant.

The present system promises durability.   If any danger assails it, it is the absorption of power into one gigantic mass, which would triumph for a while, then crumble beneath its weight.

In the consideration of this Question, it will be the most candid and satisfactory method to take a comprehensive review of all the legislative powers granted by the Constitution ; for to reason from detached passages will be ever inconclusive, and liable to mislead the mind into a labyrinth of uncertainty and error.

The legislative power of the Federal Government is principally comprehended within the eighth section of the first article of the Constitution. The first section of that article expressly declares, that all the legislative powers granted by that instrument shall be vested in a Congress of the United States, to consist of a Senate and House of Representatives. The clause which grants to Congress the generality of its Legislative Powers, is in the following words :

Summary of the Legislative Powers of Congress.

" *The Congress shall have power—*

" To lay and collect taxes, duties, imposts, and excises, to pay the debts, and provide for the common defence and general welfare of the United States ; but all duties, imposts, and excises, shall be uniform throughout the United States :

Constitution of the United States. Article I. Section 8.

" To borrow money on the credit of the United States :

" To regulate commerce with foreign nations, and among the several states, and with
General
delegatory
clause.
the Indian tribes :

" To establish an uniform rule of naturalization, and uniform laws on the subject of bank-
ruptcies throughout the United States :

" To coin money, regulate the value thereof,
and of foreign coin, and fix the standard of
weights and measures :

" To provide for the punishment of counterfeiting the securities and current coin of the United States :

" To establish post-offices and post-roads :

" To promote the progress of science and
useful arts, by securing, for limited times, to
authors and inventors, the exclusive right to
their respective writings and discoveries :

" To constitute tribunals inferior to the Supreme Court :

" To define and punish piracies and felonies
committed on the high seas, and offences against
the law of nations :

" To declare war, grant letters of marque and
reprisal, and make rules concerning captures on
land and water :

" To raise and support armies ; but no appropriation of money to that use shall be for a
longer term than two years :

" To provide and maintain a navy :

" To make rules for the government and regulation of the land and naval forces :

" To provide for calling forth the militia to
execute the laws of the Union, suppress insurrections, and repel invasions :

" To provide for organizing, arming, and
disciplining the militia, and for governing such
part of them as may be employed in the service
of the United States ; reserving to the States respectively the appointment of the officers, and
the authority of training the militia according to
the discipline prescribed by Congress :

" To exercise exclusive legislation in all cases whatsoever over such district (not exceeding
ten miles square) as may by cession of particular
States, and the acceptance of Congress, become
the seat of the Government of the United States ;
and to exercise like authority over all places

Снар. XV. purchased by the consent of the legislature of
the State in which the same shall be, for the
erection of forts, magazines, arsenals, dock-
yards, and other needful buildings : And,

" *To make all laws which shall be necessary
and proper for carrying into execution the foregoing powers, and all other powers vested by this
Constitution in the Government of the United
States, or in any department or officer thereof.*"

Such is the general delegating clause contained in the Constitution. The succeeding
section is mostly of a restrictive and negative
nature. Certain passages of it, nevertheless,
either expressly confer, or necessarily imply, a
further extension of the legislative power. It
is, therefore, necessary that such section also
should become the subject of critical attention.

Article 1. " The migration or importation of such per-
Section 9. sons as any of the States now existing shall think
proper to admit, shall not be prohibited by the
Restrict- Congress prior to the year one thousand eight
ive clause. hundred and eight ; but a tax or duty may be
imposed on such importation, not exceeding
ten dollars for each person.

" The privilege of the writ of *habeas corpus*
shall not be suspended, unless when in cases of

rebellion or invasion the public safety may require it.

" No bill of attainder or *ex post facto* law shall
be passed.

" No capitation or other direct tax shall be
laid, unless in proportion to the *census* or enumeration herein before directed to be taken.

" No tax or duty shall be laid on articles exported from any State. No preference shall be
given by any regulation of commerce, or revenue, to the ports of one State over those of another : Nor shall vessels bound to or from one
State be obliged to enter, clear, or pay duties,
in another.

" No money shall be drawn from the treasury, but in consequence of appropriations made
by law ; and a regular statement and account of
the receipts and expenditures of all public money shall be published from time to time.

" No title of nobility shall be granted by the
United States : and no person holding any office of profit or trust under them, shall, without
the consent of the Congress, accept of any present, emolument, office, or title of any kind
whatever, from any king, prince, or foreign
State."

In addition to the preceding, some further legislative powers are either expressly or virtually contained in particular detached passages of the Constitution. Of these, the following are a comprehensive selection :

Select passages of the Constitution, enlarging the powers of Congress.

Article 2.
Section 1. " The Congress may determine the time of chusing the electors [of President and Vice-President] and the day on which they shall give their votes; which day shall be the same throughout the United States."

" The Congress may by law provide for the case of removal, death, resignation, or inability, both of the President and Vice-President, declaring what officer shall then act as President ; and such officer shall act accordingly, until the disability be removed, or a President shall be elected."

Article 2.
Section 2. " The Congress may by law vest the appointment of such inferior officers, as they think proper, in the President alone, in the courts of law, or in the heads of departments."

Article 3.
Section 2. " When [crimes are] not committed within any State, the trial shall be at such place or places, as the Congress may by law have directed."

" The Congress shall have power to declare
the punishment of treason : but no attainder of
treason shall work corruption of blood, or forfeiture, except during the life of the person attainted."

" Full faith and credit shall be given, in each
State, to the public acts, records, and judicial
proceedings of every other State ; and the Congress may, by general laws, prescribe the manner in which such acts, records, and proceedings shall be proved, and the effect thereof."

" New States may be admitted by the Congress
into this Union : but no new State shall be formed or erected within the jurisdiction of any other
State ; nor any State be formed by the junction
of two or more States, or parts of States, without the consent of the legislatures of the States
concerned, as well as of the Congress."

" The Congress shall have power to dispose
of, and make all needful rules and regulations respecting the territory or other property belonging to the United States ; and nothing in this
Constitution shall be so construed, as to prejudice any claims of the United States, or of any
particular State."

To complete the data, upon which our reasoning respecting this question must be found-

CHAP.
XV.
ed, it is also necessary to cite such additional and emendatory articles of the Constitution as relate to the immediate subject of discussion.

Addition-
al article,
3.
" Congress shall make no law respecting an establishment of religion, or prohibiting the free exercise thereof ; or abridging the freedom of speech or of the press : or the right of the people peaceably to assemble, and to petition the Government for a redress of grievances."

Article 11. " The enumeration in the Constitution, of certain rights, shall not be construed to deny or disparage others retained by the people."

Article 12. " The powers not delegated to the United States by the Constitution, nor prohibited by it to the States, are reserved to the States respectively, or to the people."*

Reasoning
from such
premises.
Such is a faithful and comprehensive summary of the legislative powers of Congress, and of the various provisions which have been made by the general Constitution. It is to be observed, that, in order to prevent the hasty and inconsiderate enactment of laws, a limited *veto* has been conferred upon the President ; which is, however, inoperative upon the concurrent determination of two-thirds of each branch of the legislature.

* Vide Appendix.

From the preceding statement it must be ren- _{CHAP.} dered apparent, that the legislative authority of the general Government is confined to certain specific subjects, and intended to promote particularly designated objects. The Constitution of the United States is the decisive standard by which we are to discover the nature and ascertain the precise extent of such legislative powers.

Adverting then to the whole of those constitutional provisions separately and collectively, from which of them shall it be contended, that Congress can claim with propriety the right of interposing its authority for the purpose of restricting the liberty of political investigation, or even for the suppression of libels?

If we reason from the general spirit of the Constitution we shall find, that the coercion of Opinion is a subject entirely foreign to its jurisdiction. It exclusively contemplates and embraces such general provisions as relate to the common interests of the Confederacy, and leaves the controul of every other subject to the legislative authority of the respective States.

The general defence of the Union is a trust emphatically reposed in the Federal Government. Accordingly it is invested by the Constitution with the right of imposing taxes, and duties—borrowing money upon the common

Chap.
XV.
credit—declaring war—granting letters of marque and reprisal—raising and supporting armies, and such other powers as are absolutely indispensible to the effectual fulfilment of such trust. It is also the only organ of communication with foreign States ; hence it was essential to confer upon it, the authority of regulating commerce—the powers of negociation, and the right of punishing offences in violation of the Law of Nations. The general interest of the Confederacy requiring that an unity of system should prevail with respect to a variety of objects of common concern, in order that mutual intercourse might not be attended with circumstances impolitic and embarrassing ; hence, the regulation of domestic commerce—the establishment of an uniform rule of naturalization— the formation of uniform laws upon the subject of bankruptcy—the coinage of money and the regulation of its value—regulation of the value of foreign money—introduction of a common standard of weights and measures—the establishment of post-offices and roads, are subjects which among others of a similar description are properly submitted to the legislative authority of Congress. Subjects of interior and local concern. Subjects of internal regulation ; in fine, subjects not delegated to the general Government by virtue of the Constitution are expressly reserved to the people, or to the Governments of the respective States.

It is plain that the restriction of Political
Opinion, or the coercion of Libels is entirely foreign and irrelative to any of the specific clauses contained in the Constitution. It is equally evident that it is not embraced by the general paragraph which concludes the eighth section of the first article of that instrument, because the generality of expression contained in such paragraph is particularly limited and confined to accompany the powers which are specifically granted ; it exclusively relates to the enaction of such laws as are *necessary and proper for carrying the specific powers into execution.* The particular clauses confer the *original* and *substantial,* the general paragraph conveys the *incidental* authority. The former relate to the subject matter of legislation, the latter is strictly referable to the means which are to be employed. The position which maintains that such general clause conveys the right of coercing Opinion, is susceptible with equal plausibility of becoming tortured into any sense ; it proves too much to be either perspicuous or valuable.

Of the clauses contained in the Constitution some are *delegatory*, and others *restrictive.* It is the office of the first to *create* and *convey* authority, and of the latter to *limit* and *restrain* it. The restrictive clauses of the Constitution cannot be creative of power so long as they speak a language strictly *negative.* They can only be

CHAP.
XV.   rendered the evidence of authority when they
express or unequivocally imply a *positive affirmation*.   If I forbid you to take Vattel from my
library, surely no construction of such prohibition can amount to a grant of taking Puffendorf
or any other book.   If my expressions are ambiguous, still they convey no actual privilege.
It is only where my words can be fairly construed into an affirmative, that they will amount to
the grant of any positive right.   Thus where the
ninth section of the Constitution declares that
" the privilege of the writ of *habeas corpus* shall
not be suspended, *unless when in cases of rebellion or invasion the public safety may require it*."
The direct and obvious meaning of that sentence
is, that in times of invasion and rebellion Congress may decree the temporary suspension of
that writ.   It is also a further construction of
the same sentence, that it confers on the general legislature the authority of deciding what
circumstances amount to such a rebellion or invasion as will entitle them to exercise the preceding power.   But, on the contrary, the third
article of the amendments of the Constitution,
which among other things declares that Congress shall make no law respecting an Establishment of Religion, or abridging the Freedom of
Speech or of the Press, is of a nature altogether
negative ; and cannot, therefore, become the
basis of any positive authority which is not contained in other parts of the Constitution.

Most certainly it cannot be contended, that previous to the adoption of the third article of amendments the Congress were possessed of power to create a national church, or to prohibit any mode of religious faith or worship. It cannot be maintained that they had a right to destroy the Liberty of the Press, or to abolish the privilege of the people to assemble and petition for a redress of grievances. Shall it be admitted, that before the auspicious period of amendment the Constitution of the United States was an odious and deprecable tyranny, and that it conveyed the most arbitrary and despotic prerogatives? That before that happy æra we were amused with the unsubstantial phantom of Public Liberty, but in reality exposed to accumulated slavery and degradation? How is it possible that sentences altogether negative and restricting can destroy the limitations of the original Constitution, or be construed into a positive enlargement and extension of authority?

The eleventh and twelfth articles of amendment expressly declare, that the enumeration in the Constitution of certain rights, shall not be construed to deny or disparage others retained by the people ; and that the powers not delegated to the United States by the Constitution, nor prohibited by it to the States, are reserved to the States respectively, or to the People. With regard to these articles, it is to be observed that they are strictly declaratory, and that they produce no alteration in the law as it in reality stood at the time of their formation. They amount to nothing more than would have resulted from a fair and regular interpretation of the Constitution: because it must ever have been a fundamental position, that the general Government is entitled to no other authority than what is substantially granted by that instrument.

It has indeed been contended that the paragraph of the third article of amendment, which declares that Congress shall make no law " *abridging* the Freedom of Speech or of the Press," necessarily implies and recognizes a right to enact such statutes to regulate Opinion and the Press as do not abridge the liberty with respect to them which was previously sanctioned by the established law. This pernicious sophism, which leads to the unlimited empire of constructive authority, demands a serious refutation. Let it be earnestly remarked, that it is the letter and genuine spirit of the Constitution, and not the mutable opinions of men, which should constitute the exclusive standard of decision. Such restrictory provisions may proceed from superabundant caution ; they may be derived from an apprehension that obnoxious pow-

ers may be challenged in consequence of an irregular latitude of construction ; and perhaps
they may frequently imply an impression on the
mind that such powers are in reality contained
in the Constitution.   Farther than this the argument cannot extend.   And even admitting
that such third article of the amendments may be
considered as presumptive evidence of the opinion of those who framed and those who adopted it, that Congress in reality possessed those
powers ; that opinion should not be taken
against the liberties of the ˏpeople.   It cannot
amount to a grant of new powers, nor can it
alter the import of the original instrument.   The
opinion of no man can change the genuine
sense and meaning of the Constitution : the original must govern.   It is a record which can
only be tried by itself.   The text is before us ;
we are not compelled to resort to any commen-
tary.

It is further to be observed, that it is exclusively the intention of the articles of amendment
to furnish additional securities to Public Liberty, and not to confer additional powers on Congress.   They can never, therefore, be taken as
the basis of authority in derogation of the original Constitution.

It has also been maintained, that " a law
to punish false, scandalous, and malicious writ-

ings against Government is necessary for carrying into effect the powers vested by the Constitution in the Government of the United States, and in the departments and officers thereof, and consequently such a law as Congress may pass."

Such doctrine evidently proceeds from a bold and licentious construction of the clause authorising Congress to enact such laws as are necessary and proper for carrying into execution the specific powers of Government, upon the ground that libellous publications tend to obstruct its measures, and even to endanger its existence.

This interpretation undoubtedly weakens the limitations of the Constitution, and destroys the certainty of its provisions. The terms " *necessary*" and "*proper*," upon which it entirely rests, are extremely indefinite ; and may with equal plausibility be advanced in justification of every exercise of authority. The preceding clauses invest the general Government with its substantial powers. The clause in question appears to have been intended only as an auxiliary to enable them to adopt such regulations as may be immediately connected with those powers, but not to enlarge the subject-matter of its jurisdiction.

The coercion of Libels is an object of the most extensive magnitude. There is no subject which more seriously affects the liberty and interests of the public ; there is none with respect to which the interference of Government is susceptible of greater oppression and abuse. If, then, it was the intention of the framers of the Constitution, that legislative authority in such cases should have been vested in Congress, is it to be imagined that they would have been silent upon so interesting a subject, and compelled the Government to rest its claim to such important authority upon a forced construction of a merely auxiliary clause of the Constitution ?

From such an interpretation Congress may claim discretionary and almost arbitrary powers in all cases whatsoever : for as they must necessarily be the judges, and judges in the last resort, of the necessity and propriety of their own measures, unless their substantial prerogatives are governed by the clauses which are specific and express, the qualities of precision and certainty must be eternally banished from the Constitution.

The coercion of Libel is rather a subject of domestic superintendance, than an object which properly relates to the general interests of the Union. Wherever such Coercion is proper or necessary, our State legislatures and tribunals are possessed of sufficient authority to remedy the evil. It is, therefore, to be presumed to have been intended that the States respectively should solely exercise the power of controuling the conduct of their own citizens in such cases: for had it been intended to confer upon Congress a jurisdiction over Libels, why were they not mentioned as well as Treason, Piracy, counterfeiting the securities and current coin of the United States, or any other crime ?

Moreover, the words " *necessary*" and "*proper*," are of a texture too slight and equivocal to form the basis of definite and substantial authority. All the purposes for which the powers of Congress are created, are specific and express ; and it is exclusively to effectuate such purposes that those powers are granted. The position, that it is necessary or proper Congress should possess the authority of punishing Libels to enable them to carry their specific powers into execution, is only founded in speculation and conjecture. No conclusive reasoning has been advanced upon the subject. It cannot be advanced. The idea is merely founded upon vague opinion. What one individual may conceive necessary and proper, another may deem the contrary. Should Congress ever claim the most arbitrary prerogatives, upon the same lax and equivocal ground of propriety or expediency, it would be utterly impossible to resist their pretensions.

If the general doctrines of this work are founded in Truth, it is evident, that the coercion of
Libel on the part of the general Government is
unnecessary and improper : for in a community
so enlightened as the United States, it is scarcely imaginable that any misrepresentation of public measures should be enabled to defeat the beneficial purposes of administration ; and if any
overt act of resistance should take place, or any
improper combination exist, it undoubtedly possesses sufficient energy and vigilance to crush
the evil before it advances to an alarming extent.

But it has been contended, " that under such
general clause Congress has already enacted
laws for which no express provision can be
found, and of which the constitutionality has
never been questioned." A stronger consideration against the propriety of the doctrine, it
would be impossible to adduce. It exhibits, in
an irresistible light, the danger of constructive
powers ; and evidently proves, that one violation of the Constitution will ever be the foundation and the prelude of another. Let the Constitution itself be the standard of decision ; and
let us beware how we " travel out of the record." It is advice which flows from the masterly pen of JUNIUS, " never to suffer an invasion of the political Constitution, however mi-
nute the instance may appear, to pass by with-

CHAP.
XV.
out a determined persevering resistance.   One precedent creates another.   They soon accumulate and constitute law.   What yesterday was Fact, to-day is Doctrine.   Examples are supposed to justify the most dangerous measures ; and where they do not suit exactly, the defect is supplied by Analogy.—Be assured that the laws which protect us in our Civil Rights, grow out of the Constitution, and that they must fall or flourish with it."

II. *Have the Courts of the United States, Constitutional Jurisdiction in cases of Libel ?*

The following, is a summary of the Judicial Powers contained in the Constitution.

Constitution of the United States.
Article 3. Section 1.
" The judicial power of the United States, shall be vested in one supreme court, and in such inferior courts as the Congress may from time to time ordain and establish.   The judges, both of the supreme and inferior court, shall hold their offices during good behaviour ; and shall, at stated times, receive for their services, a compensation, which shall not be diminished during their continuance in office."

Article 3. Section 2.
" *The judicial power shall extend to all cases, in law and equity, arising under this Constitution, the laws of. the United States, and treaties made, or which shall be made, under their au-*

thority ; to all cases affecting ambassadors, other
public ministers, and consuls ; to all cases of
admiralty and maritime jurisdiction ; to controversies to which the United States shall be party ; to controversies between two or more States,
between a State and citizens of another State,
between citizens of different States, between citizens of the same State, claiming lands under
grants of different States, and between a State,
or the citizens thereof, and foreign States, citizens, or subjects."

" In all cases, affecting ambassadors, other
public ministers, and consuls, and those in which
a State shall be party, the supreme court shall
have original jurisdiction. In all the other cases before mentioned, the supreme court shall
have appellate jurisdiction, both as to law and
fact, with such exceptions, and under such regulations, as the Congress shall make."

" The trial of all crimes, except in cases of
impeachment, shall be by jury : and such trial
shall be held in the State where the said crimes
shall have been committed ; but when not committed within any State, the trial shall be at
such place or places, as the Congress may by
law have directed."

"Treason against the United States, shall consist only in levying war against them, or in
adhering to their enemies, giving them aid and comfort. No person shall be convicted of treason unless on the testimony of two witnesses to the same overt act, or on confession in open court."

"The Congress shall have power to declare the punishment of treason : but no attainder of treason shall work corruption of blood, or forfeiture, except during the life of the person attainted."

"This Constitution, and the laws of the United States *which shall be made in pursuance thereof*, and all treaties made, or which shall be made, under the authority of the United States, shall be the supreme law of the land : and the judges, in every State, shall be bound thereby, any thing in the Constitution or laws of any State to the contrary notwithstanding."*

"The judicial power extends to all cases in law and equity, *arising under the Constitution and laws of the United States*." Let it be enquired, whether the Constitution has invested the federal judiciary with the cognizance of Libels? and whether the laws of the United States

---

* Vide Appendix.

can afford them jurisdiction, unless such juris- ^{CHAP.} diction is comprised within the specific provi- sions of the Constitution ?

It is perceptible from a perusal of the preceding passages of the Constitution, that the jurisdiction thereby created, is of a circumscribed and particular nature, and exclusively confined to such objects, as by the spirit and genius of our political system, are entrusted to the general Government. It is evident from a contemplation of the nature of our Constitution, that the Federal Government does not possess *general* or *universal*, but is only entrusted with *limited* and *particular* powers. The extent of those powers must be gathered from the purposes for which it was instituted ; for whatever authority is not delegated, still appertains to the legislature of the respective States, or to the people.

It is apparent that the judicial power does not extend to Libels, unless they constitute one of those cases in law or equity which arise under the Constitution and laws of the United States ; for it is certain that such jurisdiction cannot be created by the clause which respects " *Controversies to which the United States shall be a party.*" Those controversies only relate to cases in which the substantial rights or interests of the Union are concerned ; and if it was presumed that the sentence, " all controversies in which the United States shall be a party," extended to create a Criminal Jurisdiction, and to vest a cognizance in the Federal Court of all public prosecutions commenced in the name of the Government, such construction would embrace every species of offence ; and by investing those courts with universal Criminal Jurisdiction, entirely destroy the limitations, and alter the system of the Constitution.

What are we to understand by the laws of the United States ? Most undoubtedly such acts of legislative authority as are sanctioned by the Constitution ; such legislative provisions as are made by Congress in pursuance of the authorities invested in them by that instrument. Certain subjects of superintendance have been entrusted to the general Government : nothing foreign or separate from such subjects, can possibly become the Law of the United States.

Much has lately been said with respect to the common law of the United States. The common law of England is an universal code, founded in immemorial custom and usage, and extending or supposed to extend to every case civil, criminal, or political in which their acts of Parliament are silent. That code or certain parts of it, has indeed been adopted in each of the States with very little variation. The State of New-York (for instance) by a particular pro- vision in their Constitution, declared that such parts of the common law as obtained on the 19th of April, 1775, except what was repugnant to that Constitution, should be considered as a part of the laws of the State. The Government of the United States is of recent original. It is not invested with the powers of *general*, but only of *specific* and *particular* regulation. How far the United States *as such* can possess a system of common law relating to their general Government, is extremely to be questioned. At all events, only such parts of the common law can obtain, as relate to the particular subjects which are within the powers of the general Government. Farther it cannot possibly extend. If the Constitution of the United States does not particularly invest the Federal Court with cognizance in cases of Libel, they can have no right to usurp it under the idea of a Common Law Jurisdiction.

It has been strenuously maintained, that the legislative authority of Congress does not extend to Libels. If such position be true, it is impossible that the judiciary should possess cognizance of such cases. No political maxim can be more universal, than that the legislative power should be at least co-extensive with the judicial; for if it should be admitted that a Judge may decide upon subjects with respect to which no powers of legislation exists, the legislature would be rendered subordinate to the judiciary, and the errors of existing laws would be placed beyond the reach of remedy.

To conclude—It appears to be the most rational opinion, that the powers of the general Government do not extend to the coercion of Libel ; and that the restriction of Public Opinion, independent of the pernicious consequences to which it is subject, is entirely foreign from the genuine purposes of its institution. The contrary position extends the empire of Constructive Authority to a height which is dangerous to the existence of a Free Republic, and repugnant to the idea of a Limited Constitution. We should always remember that one of the most invaluable advantages of a Written Constitution is the certainty with which it designates the powers of a Government, and that the best security it furnishes to Liberty is the perspicuity of its provisions. Its principal and its only use is to mark with precision the boundaries of Authority. It is the true palladium of freedom, and at once the charter of the people and the Government. It says to the former " behold your Rulers and your Laws." Its language to the latter is " thus far shall ye go and no farther." It must be obvious, that the doctrine of Constructive Authority is not only dangerous, but that it entirely subverts the original

design of such a Constitution.   Our present political system is truly excellent and beautiful.
It is only by the introduction of repugnant theories that its features can be distorted and de-
formed.   Let us cherish and preserve it.   Let
us guard the sacred text against interpolations
and commentaries : for if deprived of the amiable and interesting Original, we shall become
presented with an odious and miserable Carica-
ture.

CHAPTER XVI.

Upon the Press, considered as a vehicle of Communication.

Its importance—Its peculiar advantages in the discussion of subjects—Its influence upon Government, manners, and morals—Subject to be influenced by Government.   Danger arising from criminal coercion—Doctrine respecting Libels—Its injustice—Public and private prosecutions for Libels—The latter sufficient to answer every salutary purpose—Remarks of Lord Lyttleton—On licensing the Press—Additional remarks of Lord Lyttleton.

N EXT to the invention of Language and of Letters, that of Printing may justly be considered as the most powerful benefactor of mankind.   Before this important and valuable discovery, whatever may have been the attainments of a few distinguished individuals, the

CHAP.
XVI. great majority of the human race were destined to remain unenlightened and uninformed. It is true that in the Grecian States, particularly *Athens,* where the territory was confined, and the form of Government popular, the schools of the Philosophers, and the constant habit of political discussion, diffused a considerable portion of light and knowledge among the citizens. It is nevertheless to be observed, that the information disseminated by the schools, or acquired at the public assemblies, was neither so correct nor so extensive as that which is capable of being conveyed through the medium of the Press. The Athenians were perpetually subject to be misled by the insinuating art and dangerous subtleties of their Orators, a sprightly sally of the Imagination, a brilliant stroke of Wit, or an animated address to the Passions, too often inflamed the minds and governed the measures of that ardent and lively people.*

---

* The vivacity of the Athenians was frequently undistinguishable from Levity. The following are remarkable instances : " A whole assembly was once seen to rise and run after a little bird that ALCIBIADES, when young, speaking for the first time in public, had inadvertently suffered to escape from his bosom."—LEON, ambassador from Byzantium, whose personal appearance was of the most unfavorable kind, attempted to address the Athenians. At sight of him, they burst into such violent fits of laughter, that he could scarcely obtain a moment's silence. At length he said, " What would you say then did you but see my wife ? She hardly reaches to my knees. Yet, little as we are, when we disagree, the City of Byzantium is not large enough to hold us." This trifling " pleasantry was so successful, that the Athenians immediately granted the succours he came to solicit."

Anacharsis's Travels.

If we turn our attention to the situation of the European States previous to the introduction of Printing, we shall find ourselves surrounded by a dark and dismal gloom. The northern barbarians, who over-ran and destroyed the Empire, not content with waging war against the inhabitants and the Governments which were the unhappy victims of their fury, endeavoured to extirpate every vestige of civilization and the sciences. The establishment of the Feudal System, which followed as the consequence of their victories, produced an astonishing revolution in the manners, condition, and character of Society. After this, the annals of many centuries present a miserable spectacle of universal ignorance and oppression. If at distant intervals we behold a solitary gleam of light, we are constrained to lament that its unavailing lustre is extinguished by the impenetrable darkness with which it is surrounded. To the Clergy, and even to the regular orders, it is but candid to confess that the Republic of Letters is indebted in many obligations. Imbued with an ardent thirst of knowledge, and a vigorous curiosity, those venerable men were industrious to collect the scattered writings of the Fathers of the Church, and such remains of the ancient Poets and Philosophers as had escaped the general wreck. And if their glories were obscured by the insubstantial subtleties of metaphysical and polemic disputation, it must nevertheless be ac-

CHAP.
XVI.
knowledged that such disputation contributed to expand the powers of Intellect ; and that to the labours of the schoolmen, we must in a great measure attribute the revival of Learning. Still the condition of society was rude and unenlightened, until the introduction of the Press afforded a new and powerful spring to human genius and activity. From this auspicious period we may date a constant succession of able writers in every department of Science, whose labours, instead of being confined to the possession of a few, have been attended with extensive circulation. The smaller periodical publications, devoted to general improvement, are entitled to particular consideration : the trifling expence at which they are procured, and the intelligible method in which they treat their subjects, render them peculiarly serviceable to those whose circumstances are limited, and whose time is chiefly occupied by necessary labour. To the Press, therefore, we are indebted for the most inestimable benefits. It will secure the Knowledge which is now extant, and perpetuate all the improvements which succeeding ages shall produce. With facility it multiplies the copies of Literary Productions, affords to Learning a more general and extensive dissemination, and becomes the useful Instructor of the people. In fine, it is a sacred pledge for the progressive improvement of the human race, and an eternal

barrier against the rude attacks of future Goths CHAP. XVI.
and Vandals.

As a vehicle of information the Press is possessed of peculiar advantages. The rapidity of
oral addresses—the declamatory stile, impas-
sioned manner, and intemperate gesture of the
Orator—may arrest the Imagination and enlist
the Passions: but whatever is presented to us
in Print is less alloyed with any circumstance
unconnected with its merits. Reason has time
to operate, and Truth an opportunity to be enforced. We have leisure to meditate and examine. If our attention has been diverted from
the speaker, or we have mistaken his sentiments, our loss in the one case, and our error
in the other, is not to be repaired: but the
printed volume is ever open to our view; we
can ponder upon its contents at leisure, and remove our hasty impressions. The latter, therefore, is more favorable to the propagation of
Truth, and less liable to become converted into
a pernicious engine of Design.

Its peculiar advantages in the discussion of subjects.

The Press is undeniably possessed of extensive influence upon Government, Manners, and
Morals. Every exertion should, therefore, be
employed to render it subservient to Liberty,
Truth, and Virtue. While Society is furnished
with so powerful a vehicle of Political Information, the conduct of administration will be more

Its influence upon Government, Manners, and Morals.

cautious and deliberate : it will be inspired with respect towards a Censor whose influence is universal.   Ambition cannot fail to dread that vigilant guardian of Public Liberty, whose eye can penetrate, and whose voice be heard, in every quarter of the State.

It may not be considered as a whimsical speculation to remark, that the introduction of a Press particularly harmonizes with the establishment of the Representative System.   That community, whose Government is administered by the wisest and most virtuous men it possesses, has certainly attained the *acme* of political perfection.   When Learning was more rare and confined than it is at present, there must certainly have existed a greater aristocracy of Talents.   Such, indeed, is the aristocracy which Nature and Justice will ever dictate.   Eminent abilities, when united to Probity, are undoubtedly entitled to superior influence.   It is the tendency of the Press to render intellectual acquirements more general.   The light it diffuses will continually increase the number of accomplished individuals, and enable Society to select and distinguish Merit.   The Press is, therefore, an excellent auxiliary to promote the progressive perfection of the Representative System.

It cannot be denied that the Press maintains a powerful influence over Manners and Morals.

An instrument which so extensively dissemi-
nates Opinion, and which is so eminently qualified for Argument and Ridicule, cannot fail to
produce a general and powerful effect. Ridicule, indeed, should never be considered as a
test of Truth : but yet, it may be successfully
applied in exposing Folly, and combating what
may be termed the Minor Vices. Argument,
however, is the most salutary and rational mean
of correcting our prejudices, and establishing
the empire of Truth. There is no vehicle better adapted for the circulation of reasoning, or
the communication of sentiment, than the Press.
There is none which is better qualified for acquiring an ascendancy over Morals and Conduct.

An instrument which is capable of becoming
prostituted to so much *Mischief*, as well as rendering such important and extensive benefits (it
will naturally be alledged) " should be carefully
confined within the bounds of Rectitude and
Virtue. While we assiduously cultivate and
cherish the valuable plant, let us at the same
time diligently prune its luxuriant and irregular
excrescences." It would, doubtless, be desirable to controul the Licentiousness of the Press,
if any means could be pursued for that purpose
without endangering its Liberty.

CHAP.
XVI.

Subject to
be influ-
enced by
Govern-
ment.

There are two opposite extremes of Error to which the Press is liable to be perverted. The one, an interested partiality towards the Government; the other, a wanton or designing misrepresentation of its measures. In each of these cases the Press may be considered as Licentious : for the evil equally consists in a deviation from Truth. Of these evils, the former is incomparably the most formidable ; because an Administration being an organized, disciplined, and powerful body, is particularly qualified to enlist in its service every Instrument that is capable of stamping a forcible impression upon the public mind. Possessed of the gifts of patronage, they have always abundant means to reward the attachment of their favorites. The candidates of preferment, that class of individuals so numerous, and so indefatigable in every community, will be constantly ready to offer the oblations of unmerited panegyric ; and there will always be more to apprehend from Servility and Flattery, than from Slander or Invective.

Every departure from Truth is pernicious. Impartiality should be a perpetual attribute of the Press. Neither Fear on the one side, nor the Hope of Reward on the other, should intimidate or influence its enquiries. It should neither be bribed to lavish unmerited applause, nor menaced into silence. The usefulness of periodical publications depends upon their steady

and inflexible adherence to Rectitude. The C<small>HAP.</small>
XVI.
moment that corrupt or foreign considerations
are suffered to bias, or to stain their pages, they
become injurious to the genuine interests of
Society.

Why should we examine only one side of the
picture ? Why this extreme solicitude to shield
a Government from Licentiousness, and yet this
lethargic inattention to the poison which lurks
in Flattery ? Is it not a real calamity when destructive Vice and Ambition become courted in
the language of adulation, and their enormities
varnished by the sycophantic delusions of panegyric ? Is Liberty but a sounding name ; and
have Truth and Justice no substantial existence ? Let us consider things as they are. It
is proper that upon all occasions our decision
should be governed by Experience. In every
community in which the Press has been established, there have always been a greater number of periodical papers implicitly devoted to
cabinet interests, than those which have been
opposed from views extraneous to Rectitude.
As far as undue influence has been engaged in
the discussion of political subjects, the balance
of partiality has evidently preponderated on the
side of Government. If any additional check is
wanting, it is for the protection of the People,
and not for the preservation of Authority.

But what is the remedy proposed to correct
the Licentiousness of the Press? The coercion
Danger of of a Penal Code, to be applied at the discretion
criminal
coercion. of the Government! Informations and criminal
prosecutions, at the instance and pleasure of Public Officers! Can it be possible that there is nothing
to apprehend from such vindictive and rigorous
proceedings? Can the character of such restrictive system be rescued from the imputation of extreme partiality? Shall we punish for unmerited
censure, and yet excuse the most false and un-
deserved adulation? Shall we stigmatize the
man who dares to condemn, and yet protect the
venal parasite who would betray his country
from base and sordid views? Shall we entrench
and fortify the powers of Prerogative, but remain regardless of the security of Public Liberty?

If there is any truth in the reasoning contained in the preceding Chapters, we may securely
trust to the wisdom of Public Opinion for the
correction of Licentiousness. It has already
been maintained, that the general sentiment is
the only powerful check against the encroach-
ment of Ambition, and the only salutary guardian of the Rights of the People; that the effi-
cacy of this sacred Preservative can only be
maintained so long as its situation is independent; and that, therefore, no power whatever
should be suffered to intimidate or controul it.

It has also been maintained that penalties are _{CHAP.} continually liable to become an engine of oppression, and to prevent the deliberate and unembarrassed formation of Public Opinion;—that a Government, founded upon the adamant of political truth, has nothing serious to apprehend from the feeble shafts of Misrepresentation ;—and that the penetration of Society, continually improving in accuracy by the habit of investigation, will be a sufficient safeguard against all the evils apprehended from Licentiousness.

It is essential to examine the prominent principles of the present doctrine of Libels, in order that we may accurately appreciate the grounds upon which it is usually vindicated. Its first proposition is, that in criminal prosecutions *the tendency which all Libels have to foment animosities, and to disturb the public peace, is the sole consideration of the law ;* and that it is, therefore, perfectly immaterial, with respect to the essence of a Libel, whether the matter of it be true or false—since the *provocation*, and not the *falsity*, is the thing to be punished criminally.*

In the first place, it is to be observed, that agreeably to such doctrine the exclusive consideration of the Law rests upon a circumstance

* Blackstone's Commentaries, v. iv. p. 150.

entirely foreign to the intrinsic merits of the subject.   Its sole attention is confined to the preservation of the public peace ; and its principal
pretext is, that the criminal coercion of Libels
is indispensible to the maintenance of general
tranquility.   Inasmuch, therefore, as every publication which severely animadverts upon the
conduct of any individual, or upon the measures
of Government, whether it be founded in truth
or falsehood, is presumed to have a tendency to
disturb the public peace, in the eye of the Law
it is equally a Libel, and its Author exposed to
punishment.

Its injus-
tice.   Truth can never be a Libel. The system which
maintains so odious a proposition, is founded in the most palpable injustice.   Its obvious
consequence is to render the political magistrate
inviolable, and to protect him from punishment
or animadversion, even for the greatest enormities.   Wherever such a doctrine obtains, there
is an end to Freedom and to Justice.   In the
most atrocious oppression that can be exercised
by Government, according to such theory, there
will be the greatest necessity for silence and
concealment.   As the most aggravated injuries
to the community will be the most calculated to
kindle popular resentment and indignation, a
regard to public tranquility will require that
every publication with respect to them should
be suppressed.   As the well grounded com-

plaint will be more likely to foment disturban- Chap. XVI.
ces than the unfounded tale of Calumny, the
greater the Truth, the greater will be the Libel.
If Truth is pronounced to be a Libel, can it be
said that the Press possesses freedom, or that it
is a check against the encroachments of Power?
To maintain such doctrine, is to declare open
war against Political Enquiry, entirely destroy
the responsibility of the Magistrate, and establish the throne of Absolute Despotism upon
the ruins of Civil Liberty.

Criminal prosecutions for Libels can never be
necessary to preserve the public tranquility : the
coercion of Violence is abundantly sufficient for
that purpose. It is requisite, indeed, that the
laws should be positive and stern with regard to
every act of open disorder. Nothing more can
be required.—Let the punishment of every
breach of the peace be severe and certain ; let
it be universally understood that intemperate
conduct will inevitably expose the aggressor to
penalty : individuals will, in such case, abstain
from Violence, for the same reasons that they
abstain from any other offence ; and it may be
pronounced, with confidence, that sufficient security is interposed for the preservation of tranquility.

Independent of its pernicious tendency in
other respects, the present system of Libel is

therefore unnecessary for the preservation of order in Society.   It perpetually implies a want
of confidence in the energy of the law, and conveys an impolitic acknowledgment of the imbecility or the insincerity of Government.   It tells
us that the Civil Magistrate is too impotent to
suppress the ebullitions of Wrath, and must
therefore act the tyrant over Truth.   If a public
officer has been rendered an object of sarcasm,
shall it be admitted that he will be so regardless
of the dignity of Character as to yield to the intemperate violence of Passion?   If so, let him
be punished in an exemplary manner.   Suppose
that a Libel has been published concerning a
private individual, shall it be acknowledged
that the laws are too feeble to restrain him within the bounds of moderation?

With what sentiments should we listen to a
Judge, who, in a solemn and deliberate address
to a Jury, should tell them, " Gentlemen, under the sacred obligation of an oath, you have
pledged yourselves to try the defendant for a
Libel.   It is a matter of extreme indifference
whether he has published Truth or Falsehood :
it is enough that he has published.   Although
every sentence he has printed be true, still is he
guilty of a crime.   By your verdict you must
condemn him.   It is my province, and within
my discretion, to fix the measure of his punishment."

"Your enquiries are altogether foreign to the jurisdiction of Justice. It is the policy of the State that even Truth herself should be punished. Her native charms; her honest simplicity, and her unspotted robes of Innocence, cannot protect her from the rigorous sentence. The public peace must be preserved. Our laws are so disgracefully imbecile and imperfect, that we cannot maintain tranquility without the sacrifice of Truth."

It would be impossible to imagine a system more hostile to morals. There is not a virtue more useful and amiable than Sincerity. It commands an incessant and inflexible adherence to Truth. It invites us to declare our opinions respecting men and manners with Candour and Fortitude. It is peculiarly favorable to the generation of excellence ; because every man will be taught to feel that his character and conduct are always open to examination, and that he will not be enabled to acquire a greater degree of esteem than he in reality deserves. There will ever exist a certain proportion of Vice, which cannot be reached by the interposition of the ordinary Judicature : for the suppression of that we must exclusively depend upon the public Censorship. What then shall we say of the system which protects such Vice by the face of inviolability, or conceals it under the mask of hypocrisy ? What will be the character of that

CHAP.
XVI. Society in which the ingenuousness of Truth, and the manly openness of Sincerity, are never to be discovered, and where every man is compelled to conceal his sentiments respecting his neighbour under the most impenetrable disguise ?

Another prominent principle of the present doctrine concerning Libels, is, that " the Liberty of the Press entirely consists in laying no previous restraints upon publications, and not in freedom from Censure for Criminal matter when published." This definition, of which the principal force consists in its excluding the idea of a previous *imprimatur*, is true as far as it extends ; but it is extremely imperfect. Of what use is the liberty of doing that for which I am punishable afterwards ? In the same sense it may be said that I have the liberty to perpetrate felony or murder, if I think proper to expose myself to the penalties annexed to those crimes. In ascertaining the rights I possess, it is not to be enquired what I may do, and be· punished ; but what I am entitled to perform without being subjected to punishment. The preceding explanation of the legal Liberty of the Press is fallacious in the extreme. It amounts to nothing definite. It cannot be said that any Liberty of the Press is established by law, unless the publication of Truth is expressly sanctioned, and it is particularly ascertained what species of writings shall be comprehended under the title of Libels. CHAP. XVI.

It is far from being maintained that Slander should be suffered to exist with impunity. On the contrary, it is admitted, that rational and judicious measures should be taken to deprive it of its sting. But it is contended, that private prosecutions, at the suit of the injured party, are sufficient to answer every beneficial purpose, and will entirely supercede the necessity of criminal coercion.

Public and private prosecutions for Libels.

To criminal prosecutions for Libels there will always exist the most serious objections. They are invariably, more formidable than the evil they are intended to prevent. As a security to a virtuous administration, they can never be necessary. In the hands of a vicious minister, they will be prostituted to the most pernicious purposes.

In such prosecutions the defendant must seldom expect the benefit of a fair and impartial trial by Jury. In seasons which require the most unshaken constancy and fortitude, there will always be the most to apprehend from the servility or the tyranny of Judges. When Ambition and Hypocrisy become seated in the cabinet, they will generally have the address to

select a LAUD to profane the pulpit, and a
JEFFERIES to prostitute the independence of
the bench. If it is the wish of Government
that the accused should be condemned, it is
not to be expected that such inclination should
become resisted. The Judiciary will possess a
common spirit with the Executive ; and by
every undue method endeavour to mislead, or
to intimidate the Jury. It is seldom, indeed,
in such cases, that the real merits of the question are determined by the latter. Notwithstanding it is true that Juries have the constitutional right of returning a general verdict (that
is to decide as well upon the *law* as the *facts*
which relate to the trial) this right is generally
discouraged by Courts, and seldom exercised by
Jurors. In the prosecutions for Libels it is held
to be the province of the Jury to ascertain the
fact of publication, and that of the Court to determine whether such publication is libellous or
not. Now it rarely happens that the fact of
publishing will admit of dispute : the substantial
enquiry is confined to the criminal contents of
the writing. The consequence of such doctrine
is, therefore, in effect to deprive the defendant
of a trial by Jury, and subject him to the sole
decision of the Judge : for as the real merits of
the cause, and the principal question to be determined, respects the interpretation of the publication, the Court, and not the Jury, is in reality the Tribunal which pronounces upon the

subject, and decrees the punishment to be inflicted.

Civil prosecutions, at the suit of injured
individuals, are a sufficient restraint upon the
licentiousness of the Press.   As in such prosecutions it is left to the Jury to ascertain the da-
mages sustained, while they afford a real compensation for the injury, they are much less likely to be rendered a dangerous weapon in the
hands of a prevailing party, or an aspiring administration.   Such forum is, therefore, abundantly sufficient to answer every valuable purpose.   It is competent to inflict a sufficient punishment upon the malignant Slanderer, and to
afford an adequate satisfaction to him who has
been unjustly stigmatized.   But suppose that
an Officer of Government has been an object of
malevolence; what difference should that circumstance occasion? Undoubtedly none.   Let
the Officer be placed upon the same footing
with a private individual.   The character of
every man should be deemed equally sacred,
and of consequence entitled to equal remedy.
The punishment will be uniform, and the motives to abstain from aspersion will be the same
in both cases.   An impartial Jury of Citizens
are as competent to decide upon the provocation which has been given, and the retribution
it demands, as the most arbitrary tribunal; and
the injured individual, whether he fills a public,

CHAP.
XVI. or is confined to a private station, will have as
little incentive to acts of turbulent aggression as
if his wrongs were redressed by the terrors of a
Starchamber, or the barbarity of an Inquisition.

As far as the interests of Government, in its
collective capacity are concerned, it has been a
principal object of this work to prove, that no
necessity can exist for the criminal suppression
of Libel.   It is impossible that State prosecutions should not be dangerous to the Liberty of
the Press ; while, on the other hand, the penetration which is justly to be ascribed to Public
Opinion, will always be a sufficient preservative of the powers of the Civil Magistrate.

Remarks
of Lord
Lyttelton.
It is forcibly observed in the works of Lord
LYTTLETON, that " in a free country the Press
may be very useful as long as it is under no partial restraint : for it is of great consequence that
the people should be informed of every thing
that concerns them ; and, without printing,
such knowledge could not circulate either so
easily or so fast."

" To argue against any branch of Liberty
from the ill use that may be made of it, is to
argue against Liberty itself, since all is capable
of being abused.   Nor can any part of Freedom
be more important, or better worth contending
for, than that by which the spirit of it is *preserv-*

ed, supported, and *diffused.* By this appeal to CHAP. the judgment of the people, we lay some re- XVI. straint upon those ministers who may have found means to secure themselves from any other *less incorruptible tribunal ;* and sure they have no reason to complain if the public exercises a right which cannot be denied without avowing that their conduct will not bear enquiry. For though the best Administration may be attached by Calumny, I can hardly believe it would be hurt by it : because I have known a great deal of it employed to very little purpose against gentlemen in opposition to ministers, who had nothing to defend them but the force of Truth."

The licentiousness of the Press has of late be- On licens-come a theme of fashionable invective : but Press. those who have been most clamorous in their philippics, have in general been most hostile to its liberty. The Press is undoubtedly a power-ful instrument ; and, when left to itself, its na-tural direction will be towards Truth and Vir-tue. It is by no means surprising that Am-bition should always be jealous of so formidable and discerning an Opponent. Under Arbitrary Governments it is a practice to prohibit every publication that has not been previously perused and sanctioned by some of its officers. By this means every writing, which is friendly to the spirit of freedom, is suppressed ; and nothing can appear but what is on the side of Govern-

ment.   By such regulations it is obvious that
the Press, instead of being a guardian of Public Liberty, is rendered a dangerous and servile
slave to Despotism.   In such case (continues
Further
remarks of Lord LYTTELTON) there should be "An In-
Lord Lyt-
tleton. spector for the People as well as one for the
Court.   But if nothing is to be licensed on the
one side, and every thing on the other, it would
be vastly better for us to adopt the Eastern policy, and allow no printing at all, than to leave
it under such a partial direction."

It should ever be remembered that the present
system of Libel, is the offspring of a Monarchy.
However it may correspond with hereditary
establishments, and the existence of privileged
orders, the dangerous exotic can never be reconciled to the genius and constitution of a Representative Commonwealth.

CHAPTER XVII.

CONCLUSION.

𝔒𝔫 𝔱𝔥𝔢 𝔪𝔢𝔞𝔫𝔰 𝔬𝔣 𝔍𝔪𝔭𝔯𝔬𝔟𝔢𝔪𝔢𝔫𝔱.

The interference of Government inadmissible—Literary associations—Intercourse of Sentiment—Vehicles of communication—Education—Office of the Preceptor—Conclusion.

W HEN we take a comprehensive review of the history of past ages, and contemplate Society as it now exists, it must become a source of exquisite consolation, to consider Man as destined to perpetual improvement. So much Vice and Misery have hitherto existed in the world, so many enormities have followed each other in uninterrupted succession, as to occasion a pernicious theory of misanthropy, and induce a belief that our species are incapable of illustrious virtues. Upon a more accu-

CHAP.
XVII. rate and philosophical survey of the subject, we
shall find that the great majority of Crimes have
sprang from artificial passions and propensities.
Avarice, Ambition, and Want, those powerful
incentives to evil, have proceeded from Society
rather than from nature.   Under the influence
of a more auspicious system, we may reasonably anticipate that the vices which have originated in the errors of Social Institution will gradually become annihilated, and that such Improvement will be the necessary consequence
of the progressive advancement of Intellect.

All our hopes upon this interesting subject,
must be centered in the activity of Mind.   The
enlightened advocate of Freedom should entirely
discard every idea of promoting the improvement of Society by force.   Man is a creature of
Education and of Habits.   That Education, and
those Habits, are of gradual and almost imperceptible formation.   Where they are pernicious,
it is necessary that they should become destroyed, in the same progressive manner in which
they were originally acquired.   No improvement can be valuable, or durable, except what
keeps equal pace with the increase of Knowledge.   The melioration of Society should commence in the melioration of Opinions, Manners,
and Morals, and not in the prostration of Government.

On the other hand, it is true, that Tyranny is uniformly adverse to Improvement. Its interference with any circumstance which relates The inter-ference of Govern-ment in-admissi-ble. to the formation of opinion, is perpetually hostile to the progression of Knowledge. The subject is of a nature too delicate and interesting to admit of any agency on the part of Government. The idea of controuling the general sentiment by any act of Authority, should ever excite the utmost solicitude and circumspection. It has been perceived that Public Opinion is that inviolable property of Society which must decide in the *dernier resort* upon every topic of general concern. It should, therefore, be continually permitted to flow in a natural and unbiassed direction. When left to itself, Truth will be the only object of its researches ; and its tendency will steadily be directed towards the public benefit. Government should in no case be permitted to abridge the independence, or controul the sentence of that which is its Judge.

Literary Associations are particularly adapted Literary Associa-tions. to discussion : but it is not to be denied that they may be rendered subservient to improper purposes. In the present state of Society they may become the theatres of intrigue and cabal. Wherever they exist their conduct should be vigilantly observed. Still an attempt to suppress them would be highly dangerous and tyrannical.

It is not until they burst out into inflammatory conduct, or exhibit violent symptoms of disorder, that the magistrate should exercise coercion ; and even then it is to be understood that the outrage, and not the association, is the genuine object of such coercion.　In proportion as Society becomes improved, the chance that associations may be directed to a pernicious tendency, will perpetually diminish.　Even at present it is probable that the benefit to be expected is far greater than the evils to be apprehended.　If Truth is more powerful than Error, it is to be presumed that it will always maintain a superiority of influence ; and should such Societies ever overstep the boundaries of propriety, or assume any degree of political ascendency, it is then only that they should be subjected to salutary discipline.

It will be affirmed, that Associations may be rendered subservient to the particular views of sectaries or factions.　Admitted.　Their opponents will have the same right and the same spirit of association.　The collision produced will be favorable to the eventual reception of Truth. The heresy of Sectarists will be sure of becoming vanquished in such a state of intellectual fervour and activity ; and Society, at length, having heard the arguments, and examined the pretensions of both parties, will finally decide the controversy.

Above all, it is necessary to social improve- CHAP.
XVII.
ment, that the intercourse of sentiment should
remain free and unrestricted. Mind should feel Intercourse of
itself at perfect liberty to act and to expatiate. Sentiment.
Nothing should be interposed to damp its ardour, or arrest it in its career. Every thing
should be left to individual vigour and activity.
Men should be completely free to communicate
their opinions as well as to receive them. Instead of being restrained, they should rather be
stimulated to pursue every topic of enquiry, and
to unite with others in such pursuit with freedom and independence.

It is equally necessary that every vehicle of Vehicles
of Com-
communication, every instrument, and every fa- munica-
tion.
culty by which Mind can correspond with Mind,
should remain entirely free from influence. The
Press, as the most important and powerful vehicle of sentiment, should remain independent
of Government, and only be subjected to the
censorial jurisdiction of Society. Public Opinion will always possess sufficient discernment
and authority to curb its tendency towards licentiousness. The establishment of a Licensor
is, of all expedients, the most dangerous. It
is to render Government the complete arbiter
and regulator of public sentiment. It is per-
mitting the constituted authorities to proclaim
" so ye must write, and so ye must believe."

But of every subject which is calculated to impress our attention, Instruction is the most interesting. Education in its most extensive signification, relates to every method by which we can acquire ideas. The mind that has grown to maturity, and imbibed the errors and prejudices which at present abound in Society, will have much to unlearn before it can rise to any eminent degree of excellence. In the pursuit of knowledge, it is necessary to proceed with caution as well as independence. A love of Truth and Sincerity should be instilled as the cardinal virtues. Rescued from the ascendency of vicious incentives, the portals of Truth will be opened to us, and we shall still be enabled to make considerable advances.

Upon the rising generation we should look with parental solicitude. Unhackneyed in the vices and the follies of the world, their minds are open to every noble and every generous impression. Every effort should be made to preserve them from sordid and selfish propensities, and to inspire them with an ardent emulation to excel in the most sublime virtues. No object and no quality but what is truly excellent should be made the source of distinction. Under the influence of a system so congenial to our nature, those passions and those springs to activity, which have been diverted from their original destination, instead of being the incentives to

vice, would direct us to the most exalted and
virtuous pursuits.

It is greatly to be wished that some salutary
expedient could be adopted to rescue the character of the PRECEPTOR from that degradation in which it is too generally held. The province of the Tutor is, perhaps, of all others, the
most amiable and useful. It is, therefore, entitled to the highest estimation. There is not a
situation in life which enables those who are
placed in it to render more extensive and interesting services. Men of real talents and philosophical acquirements are too generally deterred
from engaging in a profession which is considered with so little respect. With what temper
of mind will the giddy youth listen to the instructions of him whom he has been taught to
consider as a vulgar and low bred pedant? Let
the office of Preceptor be regarded with that
veneration to which it is intrinsically entitled.
Men of real information and valuable talents
will then engage in it from laudable motives.
No longer viewed as destructive to respectabi-
lity, some of the most enlightened ornaments of
Society may assist in the instruction of Youth,
when it does not demand the sacrifice of personal distinction. To subdue such weak and
unhappy prejudice, is, therefore, an essential
step towards the progress of improvement.

We live in no common æra. The events which have lately passed, and those which are transpiring, though attended with terrifying convulsions, are peculiarly calculated to excite the attention, and to awaken the energies of Mind. The understandings of men appear alive to every object which concerns the welfare of Society.   Notwithstanding the irritation which now subsists, we have every reason to believe that Civil Policy will finally be established in rational and dispassionate principles. Let us equally cherish a pious solicitude for the liberties of the People, and the rightful authorities of the Government.   The existence of the one depends upon the preservation of the other.   Let us cherish exalted sentiments and generous feelings; and endeavour, by every laudable method, to promote the progress of Truth and Knowledge.   The effort is noble and promising. Should we fail in the attempt, we shall still be consoled by the consciousness of Rectitude and Virtue.   Above all, let us beware of that cold-hearted Misanthropy which would degrade the Creation of THE ALMIGHTY, and with sullen malignity rejoice in the extermination of a World.

Appendix,

Consisting of the CONSTITUTION *of the* UNIT-
ED STATES, *and the* AMENDMENTS *thereto.*

W E the people of the United States,
in order to form a more perfect Union, establish
justice, insure domestic tranquility, provide for
the common defence, promote the general welfare, and secure the blessings of Liberty to ourselves and our posterity, DO ORDAIN AND ES-
TABLISH this CONSTITUTION for the UNI-
TED STATES of AMERICA.

ARTICLE I.

Sect. 1. ALL the legislative powers herein
granted, shall be vested in a Congress of the
United States, which shall consist of a Senate,
and a House of Representatives.

Sect. 2. The House of Representatives shall
be composed of members chosen every second

year by the people of the several states ; and the
electors in each state shall have the qualifications requisite for electors of the most numerous
branch of the state legislature.

No person shall be a Representative who
shall not have attained to the age of twenty-five
years, and been seven years a citizen of the
United States, and who shall not, when elected,
be an inhabitant of that state in which he shall
be chosen.

Representatives and direct taxes shall be ap-
portioned among the several states which may
be included within this union, according to
their respective numbers, which shall be determined by adding to the whole number of free
persons, including those bound to service for a
term of years, and, excluding Indians not tax-
ed, three fifths of all other persons. The actual
enumeration shall be made within three years
after the first meeting of the Congress of the
United States, and within every subsequent
term of ten years, in such manner as they shall
by law direct. The number of Representatives
shall not exceed one for every thirty thousand,
but each State shall have at least one Representative ; and until such enumeration shall be
made, the State of New-Hampshire shall be entitled to chuse three ; Massachusetts, eight ;
Rhode-Island and Providence Plantations, one ;

Connecticut, five ; New-York, six ; New-Jer-
sey, four ; Pennsylvania, eight ; Delaware, one ;
Maryland, six ; Virginia, ten ; North Carolina,
five ; South Carolina, five ; and Georgia, three.

When vacancies happen in the representation
from any State, the executive authority thereof
shall issue writs of election to fill such vacancies.

The House of Representatives shall chuse
their Speaker and other officers ; and shall have
the sole power of impeachment.

Sect. 3. The Senate of the United States shall
be composed of two Senators from each State;
chosen by the legislature thereof, for six years ;
and each senator shall have one vote.

Immediately after they shall be assembled in
consequence of the first election, they shall be
divided as nearly as may be into three classes.
The seats of the senators of the first class shall
be vacated at the expiration of the second year,
of the second class at the expiration of the fourth
year, and of the third class at the expiration of
the sixth year, so that one third may be chosen
every second year : and if vacancies happen by
resignation, or otherwise, during the recess of
the legislature of any State, the executive thereof
may make temporary appointments until the

next meeting of the legislature, which shall then
fill such vacancies.

No person shall be a senator who shall not
have attained the age of thirty years, and been
nine years a citizen of the United States, and
who shall not, when elected, be an inhabitant
of that State for which he shall be chosen.

The Vice-President of the United States shall
be President of the Senate, but shall have no
vote, unless they be equally divided.

The Senate shall chuse their other officers,
and also a President *pro tempore*, in the absence
of the Vice-President, or when he shall exercise
the office of President of the United States.

The Senate shall have the sole power to try
all impeachments. When sitting for that purpose, they shall be on oath or affirmation. When
the President of the United States is tried, the
Chief Justice shall preside : and no person shall
be convicted without the concurrence of two-
thirds of the members present.

Judgment, in cases of impeachment, shall not
extend further than to removal from office, and
disqualification to hold and enjoy any office of
honor, trust, or profit, under the United States ;
but the party convicted shall nevertheless be lia-

ble and subject to indictment, trial, judgment, and punishment, according to law.

Sect. 4. The times, places, and manner, of holding elections for Senators and Representatives, shall be prescribed in each State by the legislature thereof : but the Congress may, at any time, by law, make or alter such regulations, except as to the places of chusing senators.

The Congress shall assemble at least once in every year ; and such Meeting shall be on the first Monday in December, unless they shall, by law, appoint a different day.

Sect. 5. Each House shall be the judge of the elections, returns, and qualifications of its own members, and a majority of each shall constitute a quorum to do business ; but a smaller number may adjourn from day to day, and may be authorized to compel the attendance of absent members, in such manner, and under such penalties, as each House may provide.

Each House may determine the rules of its proceedings, punish its members for disorderly behaviour, and, with the concurrence of two-thirds, expel a member.

Each House shall keep a journal of its proceedings, and from time to time publish the

same, excepting such parts as may, in their
judgment, require secrecy ; and the yeas and
nays of the members of each house, on any question, shall, at the desire of one-fifth of those
present, be entered on the journal.

Neither house, during the session of Congress,
shall, without the consent of the other, adjourn
for more than three days, nor to any other place
than that in which the two houses shall be sitting.

Sect. 6. The Senators and Representatives
shall receive a compensation for their services,
to be ascertained by law, and paid out of the
treasury of the United States. They shall in all
cases, except treason, felony, and breach of the
peace, be privileged from arrest during their attendance at the session of their respective house,
and in going to and returning from the same ;
and for any speech or debate in either house,
they shall not be questioned in any other place.

No Senator or Representative shall, during
the time for which he was elected, be appointed
to any civil office under the authority of the
United States, which shall have been created, or
the emoluments whereof shall have been en-
creased during such time ; and no person holding any office under the United States, shall be

a member of either house during his continuance
in office.

Sect. 7. All bills for raising revenue shall originate in the House of Representatives; but the Senate may propose or concur, with amendments, as on other bills.

Every bill which shall have passed the House of Representatives and the Senate, shall, before it become a law, be presented to the President of the United States : if he approve, he shall sign it; but, if not, he shall return it, with his objections, to that house in which it shall have originated, who shall enter the objections at large on their journal, and proceed to reconsider it. If, after such reconsideration, two thirds of that house shall agree to pass the bill, it shall be sent, together with the objections, to the other house, by which it shall likewise be reconsidered; and if approved by two thirds of that house, it shall become a law. But in all such cases, the votes of both houses shall be determined by yeas and nays : and the names of the persons voting for and against the bill, shall be entered on the journal of each house respectively. If any bill shall not be returned by the President within ten days (Sundays excepted) after it shall have been presented to him, the same shall be a law, in like manner as if he had signed it, unless the Congress by their adjournment, prevent its return, in which case it shall not be a law.

Every order, resolution, or vote, to which the
concurrence of the Senate and House of Representatives may be necessary (except on a question of adjournment) shall be presented to the
President of the United States ; and before the
same shall take effect, shall be approved by him ;
or, being disapproved by him, shall be repassed
by two thirds of the Senate and House of Representatives, according to the rules and limitations prescribed in the case of a bill.

Sect. 8. The Congress shall have power—

To lay and collect taxes, duties, imposts, and
excises, to pay the debts, and provide for the
common defence and general welfare of the
United States ; but all duties, imposts, and excises, shall be uniform throughout the United
States :

To borrow money on the credit of the United States :

To regulate commerce with foreign nations,
and among the several States, and with the Indian tribes :

To establish an uniform rule of naturalization, and uniform laws on the subject of bank-
ruptcies throughout the United States :

To coin money, regulate the value thereof,
and of foreign coin, and fix the standard of weights and measures :

To provide for the punishment of counterfeiting the securities and current coin of the United States :

To establish post-offices and post-roads :

To promote the progress of science and useful arts, by securing, for limited times, to authors and inventors, the exclusive right to their respective writings and discoveries :

To constitute tribunals inferior to the supreme court :

To define and punish piracies and felonies committed on the high seas, and offences against the law of nations :

To declare war, grant letters of marque and reprisal, and make rules concerning captures on land and water :

To raise and support armies ; but no appropriation of money to that use shall be for a longer term than two years :

To provide and maintain a navy .

To make rules for the Government and regulation of the land and naval forces :

To provide for calling forth the militia to execute the laws of the Union, suppress insurrections, and repel invasions :

To provide for organizing, arming, and disciplining the militia, and for governing such part of them as may be employed in the service of the United States, reserving to the States respectively, the appointment of the officers, and the authority of training the militia according to the discipline prescribed by Congress :

To exercise exclusive legislation in all cases whatsoever, over such district (not exceeding ten miles square) as may by session of particular States, and the acceptance of Congress, become the seat of the Government of the United States, and to exercise like authority over all places purchased by the consent of the legislature of the State in which the same shall be, for the erection of forts, magazines, arsenals, dock-yards, and other needful buildings :—And,

To make all laws which shall be necessary and proper for carrying into execution the foregoing powers, and all other powers vested by this Constitution in the Government of the United States, or in any department or officer thereof.

Sect. 9. The migration or importation of such persons as any of the States now existing shall think proper to admit, shall not be prohibited by the Congress prior to the year one thousand eight hundred and eight ; but a tax or duty may be imposed on such importation, not exceeding ten dollars for each person.

The privilege of the writ of *habeas corpus* shall not be suspended, unless when, in cases of rebellion or invasion, the public safety may require it.

No bill of attainder, or *ex post facto* law, shall be passed.

No capitation, or other direct tax, shall be laid, unless in proportion to the *census,* or enumeration herein before directed to be taken.

No tax or duty shall be laid on articles exported from any State. No preference shall be given by any regulation of commerce or revenue to the ports of one State over those of another : nor shall vessels bound to, or from one State be obliged to enter, clear, or pay duties in another.

No money shall be drawn from the treasury, but in consequence of appropriations made by law ; and a regular statement and account of the

APPEN-
DIX. receipts and expenditures of all public money shall be published from time to time.

No title of nobility shall be granted by the United States; and no person holding any office of profit or trust under them, shall, without the consent of the Congress, accept of any present, emolument, office, or title, of any kind whatever, from any king, prince, or foreign State.

Sect. 10. No State shall enter into any treaty, alliance, or confederation; grant letters of marque and reprisal; coin money, emit bills of credit; make any thing but gold and silver coin a tender in payment of debts; pass any bill of attainder, *ex post facto* law, or law impairing the obligation of contracts, or grant any title of nobility.

No State shall, without the consent of the Congress, lay any imposts, or duties on imports, or exports, except what may be absolutely necessary for executing its inspection laws; and the net produce of all duties and imposts, laid by any State on imports, or exports, shall be for the use of the treasury of the United States; and all such laws shall be subject to the revision and controul of the Congress. No State shall, without the consent of Congress, lay any duty of tonnage, keep troops, or ships of war in time of peace, enter into any agreement or compact

with another State, or with a foreign power, or Appendix.
engage in war, unless actually invaded, or in
such imminent danger as will not admit of delay.

ARTICLE II.

Sect. 1. The executive power shall be vested
in a President of the United States of America.
He shall hold his office during the term of four
years, and, together with the Vice-President,
chosen for the same term, be elected as follows :

Each State shall appoint, in such manner as
the legislature thereof may direct, a number of
electors, equal to the whole number of Senators
and Representatives to which the State may be
entitled in the Congress : but no Senator or Representative, or person holding an office of trust
or profit under the United States, shall be appointed an elector.

The electors shall meet in their respective
States, and vote by ballot for two persons, of
whom one at least shall not be an inhabitant of
the same State with themselves. And they shall
make a list of all the persons voted for, and of
the number of votes for each ; which list they
shall sign and certify, and transmit, sealed, to the
seat of the Government of the United States, directed to the President of the Senate. The President of the Senate shall, in the presence of the

Senate and House of Representatives, open all the certificates, and the votes shall then be counted. The person having the greatest number of votes shall be the President, if such number be a majority of the whole number of electors appointed ; and if there be more than one who have such majority, and have an equal number of votes, then the House of Representatives shall immediately chuse by ballot one of them for President ; and if no person have a majority, then from the five highest on the list the said House shall in like manner chuse the President. But in chusing the President, the votes shall be taken by States, the representation from each State having one vote ; a quorum for this purpose shall consist of a member or members from two-thirds of the States, and a majority of all the States shall be necessary to a choice. In every case after the choice of the President, the person having the greatest number of votes of the electors shall be the Vice-President. But if there should remain two or more who have equal votes, the Senate shall chuse from them by ballot the Vice-President.

The Congress may determine the time of chusing the electors, and the day on which they shall give their votes ; which day shall be the same throughout the United States.

No person except a natural born citizen, or a
citizen of the United States, at the time of the
adoption of this Constitution, shall be eligible to
the office of President ; neither shall any person
be eligible to that office who shall not have attained to the age of thirty-five years, and have
been fourteen years a resident within the United
States.

In case of the removal of the President from
office, or of his death, resignation, or inability
to discharge the powers and duties of the said
office, the same shall devolve on the Vice-President ; and the Congress may by law provide
for the case of removal, death, resignation, or
inability, both of the President and Vice-President, declaring what officer shall then act as
President ; and such officer shall act accordingly, until the disability be removed, or a President shall be elected.

The President shall, at stated times, receive
for his services a compensation, which shall neither be increased nor diminished during the period for which he shall have been elected ; and
he shall not receive within that period any other
emolument from the United States, or any of
them.

Before he enter on the execution of his office,
he shall take the following oath or affirmation :

" I do solemnly swear (or affirm) that I will
faithfully execute the office of President of the
United States ; and will, to the best of my ability, preserve, protect, and defend the Constitution of the United States."

Sect. 2. The President shall be commander
in chief of the army and navy of the United
States, and of the militia of the several States,
when called into the actual service of the United States ; he may require the opinion, in writing, of the principal officer in each of the executive departments, upon any subject relating
to the duties of their respective offices, and he
shall have power to grant reprieves and pardons
for offences against the United States, except
in cases of impeachment.

He shall have power, by and with the advice
and consent of the Senate, to make treaties,
provided two-thirds of the Senators present concur ; and he shall nominate, and by and with
the advice and consent of the Senate, shall appoint ambassadors, other public ministers and
consuls, judges of the supreme court, and all
other officers of the United States, whose appointments are not herein otherwise provided
for, and which shall be established by law. But
the Congress may by law vest the appointment
of such inferior officers as they think proper, in

the President alone, in the courts of law, or in
the heads of departments.

The President shall have power to fill up all
vacancies that may happen during the recess of
the Senate, by granting commissions which shall
expire at the end of their next session.

Sect. 3. He shall from time to time give to
the Congress information of the state of the
Union, and recommend to their consideration
such measures as he shall judge necessary and
expedient: He may, on extraordinary occasions, convene both Houses, or either of them ;
and in case of disagreement between them, with
respect to the time of adjournment, he may adjourn them to such time as he shall think proper : He shall receive ambassadors and other
public ministers : He shall take care that the
laws be faithfully executed, and shall commission all the officers of the United States.

Sect. 4. The President, Vice-President, and
all civil officers of the United States, shall be removed from office on impeachment for, and conviction of, treason, bribery, or other high crimes
and misdemeanors.

ARTICLE III.

Sect. 1. The judicial power of the United
States, shall be vested in one supreme court, and

in such inferior courts as the Congress may from
time to time ordain and establish. The judges,
both of the supreme and inferior court, shall
hold their offices during good behaviour; and
shall, at stated times, receive for their services,
a compensation, which shall not be diminished
during their continuance in office.

Sect. 2. The judicial power shall extend to
all cases, in law and equity, arising under this
Constitution, the laws of the United States, and
treaties made, or which shall be made, under
their authority; to all cases affecting ambassadors, other public ministers, and consuls; to
all cases of admiralty and maritime jurisdiction;
to controversies to which the United States shall
be a party; to controversies between two or
more States, between a State and citizens of another State, between citizens of different States,
between citizens of the same State, claiming
lands under grants of different States, and between a State, or the citizens thereof, and foreign States, citizens, or subjects.

In all cases, affecting ambassadors, other public ministers, and consuls, and those in which
a State shall be a party, the supreme court shall
have original jurisdiction. In all the other cases before mentioned, the supreme court shall
have appellate jurisdiction, both as to law and
fact, with such exceptions, and under such regulations as the Congress shall make.

The trial of all crimes, except in cases of im-
peachment, shall be by jury ; and such trial shall be held in the State where the said crimes shall have been committed ; but when not committed within any State, the trial shall be at such place or places as the Congress may by law have directed.

Sect. 3. Treason against the United States, shall consist only in levying war against them, or in adhering to their enemies, giving them aid and comfort. No person shall be convicted of treason unless on the testimony of two witnesses to the same overt act, or on confession in open court.

The Congress shall have power to declare the punishment of treason : but no attainder of treason shall work corruption of blood, or forfeiture, except during the life of the person attainted.

ARTICLE IV.

Sect. 1. Full faith and credit shall be given, in each State, to the public acts, records, and judicial proceedings of every other State. And the Congress may, by general laws, prescribe the manner in which such acts, records, and proceedings shall be proved, and the effect thereof.

Sect. 2. The citizens of each State shall be entitled to all privileges and immunities of citizens in the several States.

A person charged in any State with treason, felony, or other crime, who shall flee from justice, and be found in another State, shall, on demand of the executive authority of the State from which he fled, be delivered up, to be removed to the State having jurisdiction of the crime.

No person, held to service or labour in one State, under the laws thereof, escaping into any other, shall, in consequence of any law or regulation therein, be discharged from such service or labour ; but shall be delivered up on claim of the party to whom such service or labour may be due.

Sect. 3. New States may be admitted by the Congress into this Union : but no new State shall be formed or erected within the jurisdiction of any other State ; nor any State be formed by the junction of two or more States, or parts of States, without the consent of the legislatures of the States concerned, as well as of the Congress.

The Congress shall have power to dispose of, and make all needful rules and regulations respecting the territory or other property belonging to the United States ; and nothing in this Con- stitution shall be so construed, as to prejudice any claims of the United States, or of any particular State.

Sect. 4. The United States shall guarantee to every State in this Union, a republican form of Government ; and shall protect each of them against invasion ; and on application of the legislature, or of the executive (when the legislature cannot be convened) against domestic violence.

ARTICLE V.

The Congress, whenever two-thirds of both Houses shall deem it necessary, shall propose amendments to this Constitution, or, on the application of the legislatures of two-thirds of the several States, shall call a convention for proposing amendments, which, in either case, shall be valid, to all intents and purposes, as part of this Constitution, when ratified by the legislatures of three-fourths of the several States, or by conventions in three-fourths thereof, as the one or the other mode of ratification may be proposed by the Congress ; provided, that no amendment, which may be made prior to the year one thousand eight hundred and eight, shall in any manner affect the first and fourth clauses in the ninth section of the first article ; and that no State, without its consent, shall be deprived of its equal suffrage in the Senate.

ARTICLE VI.

All debts contracted, and engagements entered into, before the adoption of this Constitution, shall be as valid against the United States,
under this Constitution, as under the confederation.

This Constitution, and the laws of the United
States which shall be made in pursuance thereof, and all treaties made, or which shall be
made, under the authority of the United States,
shall be the supreme law of the land : and the
judges in every State, shall be bound thereby,
any thing in the Constitution or laws of any
State to the contrary notwithstanding.

The Senators and Representatives before mentioned, and the members of the several State legislators, and all executive and judicial officers,
both of the United States and of the several
States, shall be bound by oath or affirmation, to
support this Constitution ; but no religious test
shall ever be required as a qualification to any office or public trust under the United States.

ARTICLE VII.

The ratification of the convention of nine
States, shall be sufficient for the establishment
of this Constitution between the States so ratify-
ing the same.

ARTICLES *in addition to, and amendment of,* *the* CONSTITUTION *of the* UNITED STATES *of* AMERICA, *proposed by Congress, and ratified by the Legislatures of the several States, pursuant to the fifth Article of the original Constitution.*

ARTICLE I.

AFTER the first enumeration required by the first article of the Constitution, there shall be one Representative for every thirty thousand, until the number shall amount to one hundred, after which the proportion shall be so regulated by Congress, that there shall be not less than one hundred Representatives, nor less than one Representative for every forty thousand persons, until the number of Representatives shall amount to two hundred ; after which the proportion shall be so regulated by Congress, that there shall not be less than two hundred Representatives, nor more than one Representative for every fifty thousand persons.

ARTICLE II.

No law varying the compensation for the services of the Senators and Representatives, shall take effect, until an election of Representatives shall have intervened.

ARTICLE III.

Congress shall make no law respecting an establishment of religion, or prohibiting the free exercise thereof; or abridging the freedom of speech, or of the Press; or the right of the people peaceably to assemble, and to petition the Government for a redress of grievances.

ARTICLE IV.

A well regulated militia being necessary to the security of a free State, the right of the people to keep and bear arms shall not be infringed.

ARTICLE V.

No soldier shall in time of peace be quartered in any house without the consent of the owner, nor in time of war, but in a manner to be prescribed by law.

ARTICLE VI.

The right of the people to be secure in their persons, houses, papers, and effects, against unreasonable searches and seizures, shall not be violated, and no warrants shall issue, but upon probable cause, supported by oath or affirmation, and particularly describing the place to be searched, and the person or things to be seized.

ARTICLE VII.

No person shall be held to answer for a capital or otherwise infamous crime, unless on a presentiment or indictment of a grand jury, except in cases arising in the land or naval forces, or in the militia when in actual service in time of war or public danger ; nor shall any person be subject for the same offence to be twice put in jeopardy of life or limb ; nor shall be compelled in any criminal case to be a witness against himself, nor be deprived of life, liberty, or property, without due process of law ; nor shall private property be taken for public use without just compensation.

ARTICLE VIII.

In all criminal prosecutions the accused shall enjoy the right to a speedy and public trial, by an impartial jury of the State and district wherein the crime shall have been committed, which district shall have been previously ascertained by law, and to be informed of the nature and cause of the accusation ; to be confronted with the witnesses against him ; to have compulsory process for obtaining witnesses in his favor, and to have the assistance of counsel for his defence.

ARTICLE IX.

In suits at common law, where the value in controversy shall exceed twenty dollars, the right of trial by jury shall be preserved, and no fact, tried by a jury, shall be otherwise re-examined in any court of the United States, than according to the rules of the common law.

ARTICLE X.

Excessive bail shall not be required, nor excessive fines imposed, nor cruel and unusual punishments inflicted.

ARTICLE XI.

The enumeration in the Constitution, of certain rights shall not be construed to deny or disparage others retained by the people.

ARTICLE XII.

The powers not delegated to the United States by the Constitution, nor prohibited by it to the States, are reserved to the States respectively, or to the people.

Finis.